A WALK IN OUR CLEATS

25 ATHLETES WHO NEVER GAVE UP

NFL LINEBACKER AND FAITH MOTIVATED
FOUNDER STEVEN JOHNSON JR.

WITH PAUL CARTWRIGHT

ZONDERVAN

A Walk in Our Cleats
Copyright © 2018 by Steven Johnson Jr.

Requests for information should be addressed to:
Zondervan, *3900 Sparks Dr. SE, Grand Rapids, Michigan 49546*

Hardcover ISBN 978-0-310-76760-2

Ebook ISBN 978-0-310-76761-9

Interior design: Kait Lamphere

Printed in the United States of America

18 19 20 21 22 23 24 25 26 27 28 /PCM/ 18 17 16 15 14 13 12 11 10 9 8 7 6 5 4 3 2 1

CONTENTS

THE PLAYERS

INTRODUCTION

All the best athletes have stories behind their greatness. I don't use the word *greatness* lightly, because it's very hard to be great. Like most kids, I wanted to be great . . . at something. However, too often life's struggles get in the way. So, first off, I want to thank you for picking up a copy of this book! I appreciate you taking time to read my story and those of my friends, and for opening your hearts and minds to learn that there's more to us than our stats and the jerseys we wear.

A ton of athletes in the NFL have amazing testimonies, but the ones in these pages are from guys I have been fortunate enough to know personally. It is my hope that one of these true stories gives you the encouragement and direction you need to reach for your own greatness . . . whatever that may be!

When I first came up with the idea for a book, I had no idea how to put it into action. But I knew I had an important story to tell. There were challenges I had to overcome. So right now, I want to start with a challenge for you. I want you to think about your identity. Is it the clothes you wear? Is it the car you drive, the girlfriend you have, or the respect you get from being a good video gamer? Is it the sport you play? All of these are *things*—things we take pride in, things that bring us joy and entertainment. But there is only ONE *person* who can give us our true identity: Jesus Christ.

Serving God brings us an ultimate joy that isn't defined by wins or losses, clothes or cars, friends or girlfriends. The truth is, we are not musicians, artists, gamers, or athletes who happen to be Christians. We are Christians who happen to be all those things.

Now ask yourself, "Why in the world am I good at what I do?"

When I ask myself that question, it makes me realize that, even though I may not be the strongest or the fastest athlete in the world, I have a resolve that's second to none, matched by a burning desire to be one of the greatest linebackers to ever play the game. Did I give myself these desires? Did my parents give them to me? Did the world? The answer can be confusing. So let's take the confusion out of it.

I'm here to tell you that you have a Creator in heaven. He made you perfectly. In fact, you are fearfully and wonderfully made. You possess qualities and abilities you can't describe, gifts you may not have found yet! It is God's craftsmanship that makes you able to conquer the unconquerable, climb the unclimbable, and reach the unreachable. And it is God's desire for you to spread light to others and touch the untouchable. Through God, you can do ANYTHING you set your mind to accomplish. Now, I would be a complete liar if I sat here and told you that the guys in this book, myself included, have never made a mistake. We are human, just like you. We fall short and make mistakes every day, and are tempted and prodded all the time. And unfortunately, our mistakes are often magnified and shared with the public because of what we do for a living. However, we choose not to dwell on or relive our past mistakes—we work to do better. Always remember that your mistakes do not make you. It is what you learn from them and how you move forward. That is where your tests become testimonies.

As you read this book, take your time and pay attention to our stories. Personally, I've seen God show up when I needed him most. To be honest, I almost gave up on my dreams a few times, but God has always given me enough strength to push through. Now, I'm not here to force religion on you or tell you right from wrong. But I am here to push you. I am here to give you the inspiration and motivation you need to believe that being mediocre is never an option. There will be storms in your life. You can count on that. But taking the easy road is a greater threat to your progress than dealing with the hardship head-on. This is why we grind and stay consistent. It's a lifestyle. I guarantee by the time you reach the end of this book, you will know what it's like to have an undying ambition to follow God as you follow your dreams.

Steven Johnson Jr.

CHAPTER 1

STEVEN JOHNSON JR.
Faith Motivated

@SMJ2852 Man, I look at you in the mirror every day! Ima your biggest Fan and your toughest Critic. I see you happy. I watch you cry. You work so hard, and I'm in it with you. YOU WILL MAKE IT!!!! Keep being a role model on and off the field! God is so proud of you! Just keep proving them wrong!

University of Kansas	Media, PA	Linebacker/Special Teams

A lot of people were probably surprised to see me in a Denver Broncos uniform in 2012. No college wanted me out of high school. No NFL team drafted me when my collegiate career was over. But I never stopped believing in myself and trusting God.

Now I've played more than six seasons alongside the best athletes in the world. My path to the pros wasn't typical. It was filled with disappointment. I had to overcome injuries and disbelief. But I made it by holding on to my faith. That's my message: *Stay Faith Motivated.* That's MY motto. It's what I always tell people. Even when you don't see a way out, God can help you overcome any challenge you face, even when it seems impossible!

Don't believe me?

Then you need to hear my story.

———————

No room. No scholarship. No money.

That's probably not what you picture when you think about the life of a Division I football player. But that was my reality when I woke up on a stifling hot day in Lawrence, Kansas, during the summer of 2009.

Chris Harris Jr. and Darrell Stuckey, two of my teammates at the University of Kansas, were already gone for the day. I was thankful they'd allowed me to sleep on their couch. But it was starting to get tougher to accept my situation, because I've never been the mooching type. Their house was several miles from campus, but they were letting me stay for free. And at the time, I didn't have a dollar to my name.

I lifted my 6'1", 230-pound frame off the couch and stretched. Practice was in a couple hours. I couldn't be late. No one was picking up their phones, and a bus pass was out of reach. So I grabbed my bag and started walking.

It was about ninety-five degrees that day. You've probably heard the saying, "It's not the heat; it's the humidity." In Lawrence, the heat *and* the humidity worked *together* to make summers feel like a sauna. As soon as I walked outside, the air just smacked me in the face. But I was not about to miss practice. I knew God had given me the opportunity to play at one of the best up-and-coming programs in the country. So, step after step, I trekked the several miles to the practice facility. *After all I've fought through to get here,* I thought, *man, this is nothing.*

MOTIVATED

I began playing football as a five-year-old. From the start, I excelled at the game. I earned all-star honors and was frequently named MVP of my team. Other than my dad, my grandfather was my biggest fan. He encouraged me to believe in myself. He was the first person to tell me I could play in the NFL if I worked hard and stayed on the right path. Yeah, Joseph Wootson was a huge part of my life growing up in Media, Pennsylvania. I called him "Pop Pop." Most Sundays after church were spent watching football with him. I'd pretend to be Philadelphia Eagles' quarterback Randall Cunningham by jumping over the couch with a football in my arms. He'd cheer me on.

Steven pretending to be an Eagle while his dad watched the game

>> Photo courtesy of Steven Johnson Jr.

My grandfather passed away before he saw my football dreams come true, and that hurts. He was a big reason I made it. He made me promise him that I would not smoke, would not drink, and would not turn to drugs for comfort at any time during my life. At the time I was only about eleven years old, but I promised him. Little did I know how much that promise would help me achieve my dream. And I've kept that promise to my Pop Pop to this day.

Losing my grandfather wasn't the only heartache I experienced growing up. My parents divorced when I was only twelve. From that point on, my home life was unsettled. My mom, two younger brothers, and I moved five times throughout middle school and high school. All that moving and uncertainty took a toll on me. I started giving up a bit on my love for sports. I gained weight. By the time I got to high school, kids I had once dominated on the playing field started teasing me for being chubby and a slow runner. More than once I got into a fight to defend myself. I was frustrated at my circumstances and mad that I wasn't getting considered by the varsity coaches.

Steven on his childhood teams

›› Photo courtesy of Steven Johnson Jr.

I had more people telling me that I *couldn't* do something than people telling me that I *could* achieve my goals. Many nights I'd come home crying and put my head on my mother's shoulder because I wasn't getting any playing time. I was working so hard. But at the end of the day, I felt like I was a failure. I felt like the coaches didn't like me. To be honest, they probably didn't. But God was faithful, and he showed up in his perfect time.

During the summer between my junior and senior years, one of my teammates invited me to a Bible study at the Abounding Grace Family Worship Center. I'd known about that church before, but never really cared to go. After I attended for the first time, I never missed a Bible study every Wednesday night at seven o'clock. Sometimes it was just me and two others from the whole church. But each time I went, I noticed I started to become more confident about my life. The peace I began to feel was amazing. That was when I gave my life to Christ fully and completely. Just like I promised my grandfather, I didn't turn to drugs, smoking, alcohol, or girls—I turned to God! Now don't get me wrong, I was nowhere near perfect. I made mistakes all the time. Nevertheless, my desire for God to be in my life at that time was so intentional. I was tired of being overlooked. I was tired of crying myself to sleep. I needed help.

God intervened in my life at just the right time. His timing is always perfect. I had no direction before I gave my life to Christ. But when I fully put my trust in him, he rewarded me. As a seventeen-year-old, I became faith motivated and tried my very best to live every day for Christ.

With Christ first in my life, it was easier for me to not get caught up with people who liked to party and abuse their bodies with drugs and alcohol. As my faith in God grew, other changes began to happen as well. I became more disciplined and dedicated. I started working out more and hitting the weights. As I replaced bad habits with good ones, my body replaced fat with muscle. I became bigger, stronger, and faster.

I had been a player who couldn't crack the varsity team my first three years of high school. But after practice started for my senior year, my hard work paid off, because the coaches named me captain of the team. I earned a starting spot at linebacker and ended up leading the state in tackles, receiving all-county and all-state honors. When I look back on it, I know God was the reason I had so much success my senior year. Every game was a good game. It was insane!

Though even with all the success and accolades I was earning on the football field, Division I coaches wouldn't give me the time of day. My only offers to play college football came from Division II and Division III schools. That wasn't my plan. So I turned to my pastor and mentor, Harry Jones, who encouraged me to enroll in Wyoming Seminary preparatory school in Kingston, Pennsylvania, as a postgraduate. He knew Wyoming Seminary would be a great place for me to continue playing football, working on my studies, and growing closer to God. At the same time, I could also send out more highlight film to Division I schools.

MY HARD WORK PAID OFF, BECAUSE THE COACHES NAMED ME CAPTAIN OF THE TEAM.

At first, everything seemed perfect. Five games into my first season, I had sixty-two tackles, two interceptions, and four rushing touchdowns. Colleges that hadn't even glanced at me out of high school were now interested in recruiting me. But then . . .

On the fifth play against Worcester Academy, Coach called a pass play, which had me running a flat route. It was second down and seven yards to go, and we had been making our way up the field pretty easily. But within moments, I was on the ground in excruciating pain. I knew I had hurt my left knee. I just didn't know how badly. Later, doctors told me I tore the ACL, LCL, and capsule in my knee. I watched my dad cry in anger. It was one of the worst days of my life.

My football career was over. At least that's what my coach and the doctors told me. I became depressed. Then, adding insult to injury, for some reason my coach started telling college scouts who were interested in me that I no longer wanted to play football. That wasn't true! I still wanted to achieve my dream of playing in the NFL.

But the damage had been done. Only two schools made me offers to play after prep school: Duquesne University and Robert Morris University. Neither were places I wanted to go. I was at a crossroads: I could give up on sports and pursue other talents, or I could keep trying to beat the odds.

During this time, my grandmother on my dad's side of the family told me to sleep with the Bible on my knee. We call her "Mom-Mom Marva." She was the first one to introduce me to God when I was around four years old. When my parents argued, she told me to go up to my room and keep repeating Jesus' name, believing that he would stop my parents from arguing. I didn't think God cared about me anymore, but I trusted my Mom-Mom and listened to her advice.

Through God's grace, lots of prayer, good doctors, and hours of rehab, my knee started to heal. One night, I was in tears as I sat down and wrote an impassioned email to an on-campus recruiting coordinator at the University of Kansas. The Jayhawks had wanted me to play for them when I was healthy, but backed away after my knee injury. I basically begged for the opportunity to be a walk-on for the team. In other words, they didn't have to offer me a scholarship. I just wanted to prove that I could play at the highest level of college football.

THE **ULTIMATE** ROCK

As far back as high school, I've written Psalm 18 on my cleats. This chapter has fifty verses, so I didn't write every word. But in this dope Scripture written by King David, he states: "The Lord is my rock, my fortress and my deliverer; my God is my rock, in whom I take refuge, my shield and the horn of my salvation, my stronghold. I called to the Lord, who is worthy of praise, and I have been saved from my enemies" (Psalm 18:2–3). After my devastating knee injury in prep school, this is the verse I opened my Bible to. I was feeling so down. But reading this verse again, it dawned on me: God wouldn't bring me this far to just drop me!

I wasn't sure it would work. I prayed God would make something happen, then I sent the email. What's crazy is, they replied. The Jayhawks still wanted me to come to Kansas as a preferred walk-on. I couldn't even get Division II schools in Philly to answer me, but a Division I school in the Big 12 Conference gave me a shot. I knew God was up to something.

NOT IN PENNSYLVANIA ANYMORE

That was the good news. The bad news was I'd never been to Kansas in my life and didn't know how I would pay tuition. But despite my parents' divorce, my father had stayed in my life. When he heard I'd been accepted into the University of Kansas, he mortgaged his barbershop business to help pay for tuition and other college expenses.

I sat on the sidelines most of my freshman year because of my knee. As a sophomore, I saw the field a little more, making nine tackles and recording a sack. Good teammates like Justin Springer, Drew Dudley, Chris Harris Jr., and Darrell Stuckey helped me a lot on the financial side. I had to find ways to save money and take enough credits to stay on the football team. These guys let me stay with them for free. I would shower at the football facility just so I didn't add to their water bill every month. I felt so bad about crashing with them. But I was doing everything possible to stay in Kansas.

Then, inevitably, my money ran out. Feeling like I had no options, I began to say my goodbyes. I started with my closest friends, my girlfriend, my teammates, even the family who let me eat Thanksgiving dinner at their home because I couldn't afford a plane ticket to get back home and spend the holiday with my family. Classes for the 2009 fall semester had started. I had enrolled in classes but didn't have the money to pay for them. Before I left Kansas, I decided to go to class one last time. I don't know why I went, I just knew I didn't want to leave.

Around 1:35 in the afternoon, I got a call from one of the coaches. He told me to come to the facility. I made my way across campus and walked into his office. It was then that the University of Kansas offered me a full scholarship. The coaches said I'd impressed them with my hard work and determination over the last five semesters. I felt like celebrating but, at the time, it was hard for me to believe. This same coach had always made me feel like I was nothing, constantly overlooking and belittling me.

"You dumb walk-on, you will never play here."

Steven (52) goes in to tackle Jerrell Jackson
during a game against the Missouri Tigers

≫ Tim Umphrey/Getty Images

"Miss one more tackle and I'm sending you back to Philly."

"You're working hard for no reason—go down there with the scout team."

"Why did we let you come here?"

Nevertheless, I was grateful for my scholarship. For me, it was God telling me my dream wasn't over. I now had the finances to continue my education and my football career. God had a plan. I didn't care what anyone said about me. If he wasn't done, neither was I.

Ironically, while I was on the team, there was a coaching change leading up to my junior year at Kansas. That year, I started all twelve games and led the Jayhawks in tackles. Then, as a senior, I had the best season of my life. I led the Big 12 in tackles with 124, which placed me fourteenth in the nation. As a result, I was recognized as a semifinalist for the Burlsworth

Trophy, an annual award given to the best college football player who began his career as a walk-on.

Just like in high school, I ended with an impressive highlight reel. I played in the East-West Shrine Game for the top collegiate seniors. And just like after high school, I was once again overlooked. No NFL team drafted me. Though by this time, I was used to doing things the hard way.

It wasn't that no teams were interested in me. They just didn't want to use a draft pick on an impressive but previously injured football player. In the end, around fifteen NFL clubs contacted me about signing as an undrafted free agent. I didn't know what to do. My fam-

I WAS USED TO DOING THINGS THE HARD WAY.

ily surrounded me and prayed for direction. At the same time, I was angry because I knew I was better than a lot of guys who were drafted over me. Then Chris Harris Jr. called me. My old college roommate and friend had signed with the Denver Broncos as an undrafted free agent the year before and then made the fifty-three-man roster. He wanted me in Denver and thought the Broncos would give me a legitimate chance to make the team.

Eventually, I narrowed my options to New Orleans, Tennessee, and Denver. Maybe it was Chris. Maybe it was God. Maybe it was the presence of Peyton Manning, who had signed with Denver right before the draft. But in the end, I ended up signing with Denver.

My faith carried me to the NFL. God opened the door. Now I had to work my hardest to step through that door. I showed up to training camp in 2012 with one goal: make the fifty-three-man roster. I tried to outwork everybody in drills. If my time in Kansas had taught me anything, it was that hard work pays off and you can never let anyone tell you that you can't do something.

After four preseason games, I led the team in tackles. Before the regular season even started, the Broncos offered me a contract!

I played in eleven games during my rookie year. I didn't see much time at linebacker, but I was a starter for the special teams coverage unit. On kickoffs and punts, I'd sprint down the field, try to beat the blockers, find the ball carrier, and make a tackle. Special teams can be thankless and dangerous. It's filled with high-speed collisions. But it's an important part of the game that can mean the difference between winning and losing. By 2014, *Pro Football Focus,* a respected website that analyzes all NFL player performances, named me to its All-Pro Special Teams coverage unit. It was a huge honor. One that was earned through numerous highlights, including a game on September 29, 2013.

This game was special for several reasons.

It was against the Philadelphia Eagles—the team I had grown up rooting for and dreaming of playing on. And many of my family members and friends had made the trip not only from Philly but from other parts of the country to pack into Denver's Mile High Stadium. They had come to support me against our hometown team. I knew they wanted to see me play well, but they were probably also secretly hoping for a close game.

It wasn't. Peyton Manning threw four touchdown passes for my Broncos.

Steven (53) after blocking the punt and returning it for a touchdown on September 29, 2013

›› Michael Ciaglo/*Colorado Springs Gazette*/MCT via Getty Images

The game was a blowout. We led 42–13 in the fourth quarter. Despite the lopsided score, every athlete on the field continued to play hard. With 14:05 left in the game, the Eagles faced fourth down on their own 44-yard line and were punting yet again. Time for special teams.

Wearing number 53, I ran onto the field and lined up off the right shoulder of Philly's center. At the snap of the ball, I rushed forward, pushed the center aside, and saw a clear path to the punter. Rushing straight at the green-and-white punter wearing number 8, I lifted my right arm just as his foot connected with the ball. The ball immediately hit my arm and careened awkwardly toward the sideline. I quickly changed direction, following the bouncing ball. Just a few steps from the sideline, I scooped up the ball on the 17-yard line. Surrounded by four of my teammates and 77,000 cheering fans, I galloped into the end zone for a touchdown!

The TV announcer shouted, "Fifty-three did it all!" We were ahead 48–13. Holding on to the ball, I scanned the crowd for my family, for the people who helped me achieve my dream. And they were there, celebrating my first NFL touchdown.

After three seasons with Denver, they released me. That year, the Broncos ended up winning a Super Bowl against Carolina. I tried so hard not to be bitter, but leaving Denver was very difficult for me and my family. That season I ended up playing for the Tennessee Titans, where I appeared in all sixteen games on special teams and was awarded special teams MVP. Following that season, the entire staff was fired, so I became a free agent. Then in 2016, I signed a one-year contract with the Pittsburgh Steelers. I was doing really well until I broke my fibula versus the Dallas Cowboys. I was so angry when it happened, because I was on my way to getting real reps on defense. But it put me on the injured reserve list for the rest of the 2016 season.

The Steelers re-signed me for 2017. But after one game, I was let go.

Professional football is a tough business. There are ups and downs on the field and challenges that come with trade moves and personnel decisions. Without my faith and trust in God, it would be so difficult to stay motivated.

I am living proof that you can accomplish your dreams when all else seems to be against you. Many times, I was told I was too slow and too small, but I never gave up. Being a Christian didn't make my life perfect. It didn't take away life's challenges or make it so I never stumbled. But God was with me through it all. He is a loving God, for sure.

YOU CAN ACCOMPLISH YOUR DREAMS WHEN ALL ELSE SEEMS TO BE AGAINST YOU.

Remembering how Christ lived and sacrificed to forgive me of all my sins—and yours!—helps me overcome all the obstacles I face. It also makes me appreciate the opportunities God gives me to play the game I love, representing him on and off the field. After Pittsburgh released me, I signed with the Baltimore Ravens less than a month later. I played ten games with the Ravens in 2017 and now I'm a free agent again.

God willing, I have a lot of football left to play. God has already helped me get over some seemingly insurmountable hurdles. The knee injury in prep school could've ended my career. It didn't. I got back up, worked hard, and trusted God. I ran out of money in college, but God made a way for me to keep going. Going into my seventh season in the NFL, after feeling like I would never get a chance to be a starting linebacker, I rededicated my life to Christ. With the support of my family, my beautiful wife and daughters, my passion for the game of football is at an all-time high. Continue to fight the good fight and always stay Faith Motivated. Trust me, it's worth it.

CHAPTER 2

CHRIS HARRIS JR.

The Underdog

S/O to the fam **@ChrisHarrisJr**: We been cool for like 11 years now, Jayhawks 4life, and Broncos together for 3 years. Undrafted 2 All-Pro, Top 100 & Super Bowl Champ, I'm on my way! Literally pray my hard work pays off like yours did! #StrapHarris #NoFly #StrapHaus Elite 6 All Day! Come see us! @nba2k

University of Kansas	Bixby, OK	Cornerback

Maybe it was his lack of interceptions. Despite starting every game during his four-year college career at the University of Kansas, Chris Harris Jr. recorded just three interceptions. Maybe it was the fact he didn't play for an elite college football program. Yes, Kansas is a member of the Big 12 Conference, however the Jayhawks won only eight of twenty-four games during his final two seasons.

Whatever the reason, Chris wasn't highly regarded entering the 2011 NFL Draft—despite the fact he'd recorded 290 tackles in college. That number put him second all-time in Jayhawk history! And instead of playing cornerback at the next level, scouts projected the 5'10", 190-pound athlete as a safety in the NFL. He didn't even get invited to the NFL Scouting Combine, although he certainly had the resume to earn a spot.

Not surprising to experts, Chris wasn't chosen by any team during the draft. But not surprising to Chris, he has become one of the top cornerbacks in the NFL. *Sports Illustrated* even called him the most versatile cornerback in the league. He's been named to three Pro Bowl teams and was selected first-team All-Pro in 2016 and second-team All-Pro in 2014 and 2015. In 2015, *Pro Football Focus* put him at number 4 on its list of the top 100 players in the league. And heading into the 2018 season, NFL players' votes placed Chris as the eighty-sixth best player in football.

Chris has always been an underdog. That's okay with him—just don't call him underrated. He's had faith and confidence all along that he'd become an elite NFL player.

———————

Football experts said it wasn't supposed to happen this way. The Carolina Panthers entered Super Bowl L with a 17–1 record including playoff wins. The Panthers had led the league in scoring with an average 31.3 points a game. They'd won the NFC Championship two weeks prior by 34 points! Most commentators picked the Panthers to win easily against my Denver Broncos. We'd barely slipped by the New England Patriots 20–18 in the AFC Championship game.

But at the end of sixty minutes, we walked off as Super Bowl champs, winning 24–10. Our defense dominated. We'd beaten, battered, and confused Carolina quarterback Cam Newton. He'd been sacked six times, knocked down countless others (once by me), and had his worst game of the season.

While the experts were shocked, I wasn't surprised at all. I've always believed it's not what others think that matters. All that matters is how you perform. Actions speak louder than words. We'd entered Levi's Stadium in Santa Clara, California, that day as underdogs. We left as world champions!

I've really been an underdog my whole life. I grew up in Tulsa, Oklahoma. We call it T-Town. Because my parents divorced when I was five years old, my mom raised my sister Brittany and me pretty much by herself. I remember my mom working so hard. She always seemed to have two jobs: working for the post office during the day and refereeing basketball games at night. Because she was gone in the evenings, that left me as the man of the house. I was young, but I did what I had to do to care for my younger sister. My mom was always tough on us, teaching us everything she could about discipline, organization, responsibility, and obedience.

Chris (25) tackling Cam Newton during Super Bowl L
>> Charlie Riedel/AP/Shutterstock

More than anything, she instilled in us a God-first mentality. She had me and my sister in church every Sunday to learn about God. Even if I didn't fully understand everything I heard all the time, I was always there. But knowing *about* God and having a personal relationship *with* God are two completely different things. I can't say I knew that difference as a kid, but as I got older it started to click. During my junior year in high school, I accepted Jesus as my personal Savior. After that I joined a small group of faith-minded students called the Junction Group and began to really grow in my faith.

High school was also when my athletic ability started to stand out. I earned varsity letters in football, basketball, and track. My heart was always with football, where I played defensive back and wide receiver. I was a first-team all-league selection during my junior and senior years, and I earned all-state honorable mention status after my junior season. My mom also pushed me to work hard in the classroom. I always did the best I could. By constantly focusing on my studies, I made the academic champions team my junior and senior years.

Chris (16) intercepts a pass during the 2008 FedEx Orange Bowl against Virginia Tech

>> Jared Lazarus/*Miami Herald*/MCT via Getty Images

I was doing everything my coaches and teachers said would help me get to the next level. I really wanted to play football for a top university. Growing up in Oklahoma, everybody wanted to play for the Sooners, including me. A bunch of my teammates were getting a lot of attention from colleges. Though for some reason, I was overlooked. Scouts came to a lot of our games, but for me the offers never came in. Finally, the University of Kansas made me an offer, and I became a Jayhawk.

I finished my college career with the second-most tackles in school history. Optimistic about my future playing professional football, I watched the entire NFL Draft in a room with my family and friends. We kept waiting for the phone to ring. It never did.

OPEN DOOR IN DENVER

A few days after the draft, the Broncos contacted me, wanting to sign me as a free agent. They saw me as an extra body on the practice field. I saw it as an opportunity to prove myself. As an undrafted free agent, I knew there was no margin for error. I had to play perfectly in practice to earn a spot on the roster. Nothing in me intended to return to Tulsa empty handed. I just refused to go back home.

During this time, I leaned on God a lot. I didn't understand why everything had gone down the way it did, but I knew he had a plan. I prayed for patience. I prayed to become the man God wanted me to be.

Looking back, I can see how God was preparing me, making sure I would be able to handle everything that would eventually come my way. I was learning discipline and how to stay humble when financial favor finally came. I had been waiting on God to open the right door, and he did.

Not only was it the right door, it was on the right team. When I showed up in Denver, a pair of all-time greats—Brian Dawkins and Champ Bailey—were playing for the Broncos. They were two of the most professional and successful defensive backs in the league. Once they saw I could play, they didn't care about how I'd gotten there. First-round pick, undrafted free agent—who cares! Champ and Brian wanted to win. Pretty soon they were in our coach's ear, asking him to put me in the game.

I saw a little playing time during our 2011 opening game against the Oakland Raiders. Following some injuries to other players, I got my first career start at cornerback in the seventh game of the season versus the Detroit Lions. The next week I grabbed my first NFL interception against Oakland. I finished the season with seventy-two tackles and six pass deflections. I had gone from undrafted to being selected for the NFL All-Rookie Team.

I became a starter at right corner my second season. By 2013, I'd emerged as one of the top shutdown corners in the NFL. With Peyton Manning leading us at quarterback, we went 13–3 that season. We entered the playoffs as heavy favorites to make it to the Super Bowl. We did. But once there, we lost 43–8 to Seattle. Unfortunately, I was unable to play in the game. During our first playoff game against San Diego, I tore my ACL and missed the rest of the postseason. Actually, I missed the next seven months. Sometimes I hate thinking about it. The injury occurred when I was doing a routine break, something I do all the time, and for some reason my body just gave out on me.

> **I HAD GONE FROM UNDRAFTED TO BEING SELECTED FOR THE NFL ALL-ROOKIE TEAM.**

A torn ACL is a devastating, if not career-ending, injury for some players. At cornerback, speed, agility, and quickness are crucial. You have to keep up with the elite wide receivers. Some people said my career was done and that I'd never be the same. When you were undrafted, it's easy for people to give up on you.

I had faith, and so did my family and friends. They prayed for complete restoration and a full healing. I had great doctors and physical therapists.

It took a lot of hard work and dedication, and I fought through a lot of pain and tears. But seven months later, I stepped back on a football field with my knee at 100 percent.

In 2014, I was named to the Pro Bowl team and had an All-Pro season. That year I didn't give up a single touchdown or allow a receiver to make a play of over twenty-two yards. How I play on the field is important to me. It's my job. If you're going to line up in front of me, you're going to get *strapped*. Point blank. Period. For me, that's just my No Fly Zone mentality. My desire has always been to be one of the best corners in the game. Why go out on that field to be mediocre? I work countless hours during the offseason with my trainer to better my craft. I never settle for average. I want to be the best. But I know what I accomplish on the field is only a part of the plan God has for me.

PART **OF THE** PLAN

With all the disappointment and uncertainty I've faced, I often lean on my favorite Bible verse. Jeremiah 29:11: "'For I know the plans I have for you,' declares the Lord, 'plans to prosper you and not to harm you, plans to give you hope and a future.'" All my life, I've learned to wait on the Lord. God's timing doesn't always line up with mine. His plan often looked different than how I pictured things happening. I didn't understand why teams didn't want me, but I clung to this promise and trusted in God. I knew he had a plan. *Who was I to question it?* Ultimately, God's plans have been better than anything I could've dreamt of for myself.

More important is the fact he wants me to be a reflection of Christ. To that end, I strive to be the best example I can of who Jesus Christ is. I follow him and try to treat people as he would treat them. I treat my wife in the same loving way that he treated the church. I'm not perfect, but my desire is to be more like Jesus.

God has given me a platform, and I want to use it for him. I know I'm blessed to play in the NFL and to have a beautiful wife and kids. Giving back is important to me. That's why I started the Chris Harris Jr. Foundation. I want to help other "underdogs" like me fulfill their dreams. It's also why I put on a free football camp called the Underdog Academy.

Underdogs can become superstars, even Super Bowl champs! What was David in the Bible? An underdog in an impossible situation. No one believed in him, you know what I mean? So yeah, that's something I definitely want you to know. Because with God, all things are possible.

Chris alongside teammate CJ Anderson during the Broncos' Super Bowl parade in Denver

>> John Leyba/*The Denver Post* via Getty Images

CHAPTER 3

RYAN SHAZIER

Shalieve

If it's impossible, **@RyanShazier** will make it possible!! My teammate and leader of the Steelers defense . . . fastest LB in the league . . . matches me in hard work so we good haha!! #Shalieve 4ever! #Prayfor50

Ohio State University	Fort Lauderdale, FL	Linebacker

It looked like a routine play. Cincinnati receiver Josh Malone ran a shallow crossing route over the middle of the field. After Malone caught the ball, Pittsburgh linebacker Ryan Shazier took two steps and delivered a hit with his right shoulder pad. It was an athletic play Ryan had made hundreds of times before. But this time something went wrong—and he knew it.

Immediately, Ryan reached for his lower back. He rolled over, unable to move his legs. Every eye in Paul Brown Stadium on December 4, 2017, focused on the Pro Bowl linebacker. The game stopped. He was strapped to a backboard and taken off the field on a cart surrounded by doctors, medical experts, and concerned teammates.

At the hospital, doctors determined Ryan had suffered a spinal contusion. He underwent a spinal stabilization surgery a couple of days later.

Even in the midst of this devastating injury, Ryan took to Twitter a day after being carted off the field, saying: *Thank you for the prayers. Your support is uplifting to me and my family. #SHALIEVE*

Fans holding up a #shalieve sign on December 10, 2017, the week after Ryan's injury

>> Don Wright/AP/Shutterstock

Since that time, Ryan has been uplifting everyone else. On February 1, 2018, Ryan was released from the University of Pittsburgh medical center. At first, medical professionals wouldn't comment if Ryan would ever walk again. But Ryan took to the challenge like he did to reach his goal of playing in the NFL. He immediately started rehab four times a week for two hours a day. He posted photos of himself doing pull-ups at a gym. Then on April 26, 2018, Ryan surprised everyone at the NFL Draft in Dallas, Texas.

The crowd erupted in applause and tough athletes had tears running down their faces as Ryan walked—yes, *walked!*—onto the stage to announce the Steelers' first-round selection.

After making his inspiring appearance, Ryan went to Twitter and said, *Love you all thank you. God IS SO GREAT!!!* In interviews with NFL.com, Ryan says his goal is to return to football and one day make it to the Hall of Fame. Every day is a challenge, but Ryan fully trusts God. He and his family have asked for prayers for full restoration to health. As you read this book, please pray for Ryan and his family. Ask God, the Great Physician, to heal Ryan in miraculous ways. He was told before that he'd never play football again. That was in high school. Now his determination, dreams, and faith have him focused on recapturing his on-field greatness.

"You might never play football again." More than one doctor gave this short and dreaded diagnosis to me when I was in high school. My scoliosis was so bad that medical professionals feared that my football career was over just as it was starting. Having a curved spine is a bad medical condition for a football player, but it's not the affliction I'm most recognized for.

Some fans may not know I have scoliosis, but everyone can see my bald head caused by alopecia. A beautiful, bald head is a fashion statement for men these days, but being bald as a child was a source for teasing and ridicule in the schoolyard. Kids called me "Patchy" or "Cue Ball." A lot of kids didn't realize an autoimmune disease caused my baldness. With the love and nurturing of my parents, I began to accept and proudly display my baldness. As I got older, playing in college and the professional ranks,

I even started speaking to children who suffered from this affliction to help them deal with their situation just as I did.

Ryan (in white jersey) tackling Wisconsin's Montee Ball in 2012

>> Andy Manis/AP/Shutterstock

Playing football with alopecia is no problem. Playing with scoliosis is a different story. A curved spine can develop for a number of reasons. My family worked with doctors to monitor and treat it so it wouldn't progress. And as I worked to correct the condition, I became a standout on the Plantation High School football team in Florida. At 6'2" and 205 pounds, I played defensive end and tight end. When I graduated, I was ranked by college recruiters as one of the top 25 linebackers in the country. Even at my size, I could outrun most wide receivers. I played three years at Ohio State, racking up 317 tackles and fifteen sacks, before declaring for the 2014 NFL Draft.

When the Steelers selected me fifteenth overall in the first round, I couldn't wait to start playing for the Black and Gold. Over the years, the Steelers have been tabbed with the nickname "Linebacker U." A seemingly endless string of outstanding linebackers have played for the team. Hall of Fame members Jack Lambert and Jack Ham top the list. I wanted to join this group that also includes other outstanding players like Andy Russell, Jason Gildon, Joey Porter, James Harrison, Greg Lloyd, Lamar Woodley, James Farrior, Levon Kirkland, Kevin Greene, Chad Brown, and David Little.

My goal was to be the best linebacker on the field every time I played. I worked hard in training camp to learn the system and my role on the team. From the opening-season game, I earned the spot at starting inside linebacker. A knee injury

> **MY GOAL WAS TO BE THE BEST LINEBACKER ON THE FIELD EVERY TIME I PLAYED.**

caused me to miss a bunch of games in the middle of the year, but I still finished the 2014 season with thirty-six tackles in eight games.

The next year went even better. Although I missed games with a shoulder injury, I started twelve games and made eighty-seven tackles. Then, in the 2015 playoffs against the Cincinnati Bengals, I had one of my most memorable performances. Big plays often change the outcome of a game, and I made two enormous plays. The first one came in the third quarter. We were up 15–0, but the Bengals were driving toward the end zone. Bengals running back Giovani Bernard caught a pass in the flat. I laid a crushing—but clean—hit on him and the ball came loose. Right away, I jumped on the fumble to get the turnover. But the game was far from over. Cincinnati scored sixteen fourth-quarter points to take the lead. With just 1:23 left in the game, all the Bengals had to do was hang on to the ball and run out the clock. Cincinnati running back Jeremy Hill took a handoff and ran my direction. Instead of making the tackle, I focused on ripping the ball from his arms. The ball came loose! We recovered, and then our offense drove down the field for a field goal to win the game 18–16.

Games like that make me love football. During the 2016 season, I kept up my high level of play and made my first Pro Bowl. By intercepting a pass in four consecutive games, I tied the longest streak for a linebacker since the NFL and AFL merged in 1970. I had already tallied nearly ninety tackles and had three interceptions when I suffered the freak injury against the Bengals on Monday night in 2017.

Ryan (50) taking down Frank Gore in a game against the Colts

》 John Mersits/CSM/Shutterstock

Injuries are part of football. Mine was more severe than most. I used to get mad at the Lord when I sustained an injury, but I got over that quickly. I learned that I needed to stay strong in the Lord and faithful to him. I stopped asking, "Why me, Lord?" and just stayed close to him.

I found that sometimes my injuries occurred when I wasn't being faithful to God—I was partying and didn't have my focus on him. These injuries were God's way of getting my attention and bringing me closer.

My friends also play a big part in my walk with the Lord. We text each other all the time to encourage one another. There's a strong group of Christian players on the Steelers and a great chaplain, so I have other people who lift me up and keep me accountable. I also pray with my father.

I LEARNED THAT I NEEDED TO STAY STRONG IN THE LORD AND FAITHFUL TO HIM.

He is a pastor and was once the chaplain for the Miami Dolphins. Reading the Bible, praying, and going to church or chapel with other believers is the best way for me to stay strong in my faith.

I wasn't always as close to the Lord as I am today. Although I was raised in a Christian home, I strayed from those core values after moving away from my parents and going to Ohio State. However, I quickly rededicated myself to the Lord during my sophomore year. Even though I had been baptized as a kid, I chose to be baptized again to show my recommitment to God and go public as a young man to show my renewed focus on my faith. Once I rededicated my life to God, not only did my relationships with people become better and stronger, I became a better person. As a result, my play on the field improved. I could just see and think more clearly.

Just like I threw myself into training then, I've thrown myself into rehabilitation now. Once I started getting movement in my legs, I started a walking regimen. I want to play football again. I love Muhammad Ali's quote about training: "I hated every minute of training, but I said, 'Don't quit. Suffer now and live the rest of your life as a champion.'" I used to cry on the sidelines when I was injured and couldn't practice with the team. During my recovery, I still shed tears because I so badly want to be the best player I can be.

No matter what troubles or challenges you're going through, you aren't alone. God is always with you if you make him the Lord of your life. You just gotta Shalieve!

PLAY **FOR THE** LORD

My favorite Bible verse is Philippians 4:13 (NKJV): "I can do all things through Christ who strengthens me." I'm personally driven to be the best, but without Christ's strength in my life, I fall short. Christ died for your sins. It doesn't matter who you are. Christ died so that YOU may have eternal life. He died and rose again so that, if you believe in him, you can go to heaven. God doesn't need you to be perfect when you come to him. He needs you when you are broken and humbled. Many people have counted me out, but I wouldn't be where I am today without the Lord.

CHAPTER 4

WILL JOHNSON

Iron-Willed

@Willjohnson_6 Man, whenever I watch you play, I know there is purpose behind it. We missed each other by a season in Pittsburgh. But we both have the best last name in the world. #Salute bro!! Keep grinding and keep living with purpose!!!

West Virginia University	Dayton, OH	Fullback

Fullback is a unique position on a football team. As part of the offensive backfield, the fullback is eligible to carry or catch the ball on every play. But that rarely happens. Most often, a fullback blocks. He blocks for the running back, sacrificing his body against a defensive tackle or defensive end who might outweigh him by fifty pounds. He also blocks for the quarterback, protecting the play caller from a defensive lineman or against a blitzing linebacker or a defensive back coming at full speed. To handle all the high-speed collisions, a fullback must be big, tough, and solid. He must put team success ahead of his own fame and overcome huge obstacles to do his job. He must also have the speed to break through the line with the ball, the strength to maintain possession of the ball in tight positions, and the soft hands to catch passes.

Read those characteristics again: big, tough, solid, determined, team player, fast, strong, playmaker. Put all that together and you'd be describing Will Johnson.

Will played fullback for the Pittsburgh Steelers from 2012 to 2015 before being signed by the New York Giants. During his time with the Black and Gold, he caught touchdown passes from Ben Roethlisberger and led the way as running back Le'Veon Bell racked up thousand-yard seasons.

The date was August 9, 2012. I surveyed Lincoln Financial Field in Philadelphia. The summer evening was hot. I couldn't believe how lush and green the grass turf was. As the crowd flowed into their seats, I was filled with anticipation. The upcoming game was between fierce state rivals—the Philadelphia Eagles and the Pittsburgh Steelers. I was finally going to see my first live NFL game. But I wouldn't just be *watching* it; I would be *playing* in it.

I took the hard way to the NFL. In fact, I may be the only NFL player ever to go from working as a landscaper to stepping onto a perfectly manicured field more than a year *after* graduating from college.

I was raised in a single-parent household. From a young age, I took comfort in sports. Athletics came naturally to me. Coaches and other parents encouraged me and told me how good I was. In fact, I liked sports so much that it became a detriment to my schoolwork. I didn't take my studies seriously. My grades were so bad that I was ineligible for high school sports for two years. Once I put the same effort into my studies that I did into playing sports, I was able to get my grades up and make a name for myself on the football field. During my junior and senior years at Centerville High in Ohio, I played running back, linebacker, and cornerback.

I wasn't as talented as some players, but I worked harder than most of my teammates and opponents. Hard work beats talent every time talent doesn't work hard. Colleges took notice. I received full-scholarship offers from Michigan State, Ohio State, Ohio University, and other top programs. I decided to attend West Virginia University. At the time, the Mountaineers were an up-and-coming program led by coach Rich Rodriguez.

Will brings down a game-winning touchdown catch in the final seconds of a game against West Virginia's in-state rival, Marshall

>> Jeff Gentner/AP/Shutterstock

My coaches at WVU helped me take my football skills a quantum leap forward. They channeled my work ethic in the right direction. I'd been recruited as a linebacker and wide receiver, but I converted to tight end and fullback in college. I also grew as a student. By dedicating myself to my studies, I made the honor roll as a senior.

I WASN'T AS TALENTED AS SOME PLAYERS, BUT I WORKED HARDER.

It wasn't just a physical and mental transformation I experienced in college—it was also spiritual. During my years at West Virginia, I made the decision to live my life for Jesus Christ. I grew up in the church with my mom and older brother, but in college I learned that I needed to have a personal relationship with God. I joined the Fellowship of Christian Athletes, an on-campus group that helped me with my faith. I also got involved in small groups of fellow Christians who encouraged my walk with Christ and held me accountable.

LEFT OUT BUT NOT LEFT BEHIND

Although I won many awards in college, including Offensive Champion, "Ideal Mountaineer," and was voted senior team captain, I wasn't invited to attend the NFL Combine. The combine is where every team's scouting department evaluates and rates the top college football prospects.

When the 2011 NFL Draft came, I wasn't selected. That was the same year as an NFL lockout, so I didn't even get the opportunity to showcase my talent to teams as an undrafted free agent. At first, it felt like my NFL dreams were dead. But I refused to give up. I took a landscaping job for a year while fiendishly working out and praying for God to open up an opportunity to catch the eye of an NFL club.

God answered in more ways than one. During that year, I got engaged to my future wife, Jessica. I also received permission from the Mountaineers athletic department to take part in the college's Pro Day for a second time. Pro Day is where NFL Draft-eligible players who weren't invited to the combine go through similar drills at their particular school. I showed up at Pro Day and had an even better perfor-

mance than my first year. I must've really stood out, because Steelers head coach Mike Tomlin and general manager Kevin Colbert took notice.

I got signed by Pittsburgh. Right away, I had an impact on the field. I was named to the 2012 mid-season All-Rookie Team. Later that year I scored my first touchdown, pulling in a one-yard pass from Ben Roethlisberger. I spent four great years with the Steelers. After becoming a free agent, I took the opportunity to sign with the New

Will (46) running the ball in a game for the Steelers
›› Winslow Townson/AP/Shutterstock

York Giants for the 2016 season. Unfortunately, an injury in a preseason game landed me on the Injured Reserve List for the entire season.

The odds have been against me much of my life. I didn't play a lot of high school football. I wasn't invited to the NFL Combine. I wasn't drafted out of college. I was forced to take a year off from playing the game between college and the pros. Everything indicated that I wasn't going to make the NFL. But I played five NFL seasons. God is good!

TRUST **IN THE** LORD

Proverbs 3:5–6 has encouraged me at so many different times in my life. This verse states, "Trust in the Lord with all your heart and lean not on your own understanding; in all your ways submit to him, and he will make your paths straight." In times of trial and self-doubt, it's great knowing that the Lord has a greater plan for my life than I even have for myself. Sometimes he tests us. If you stay close to him, he will reveal his plan for your life. Pray and ask him to guide your steps.

I tried to honor him with my play on the field. Every time we broke the huddle during a game, I prayed. It wasn't a long prayer, just one for protection. God wants to hear from us all the time. We shouldn't only pray during the bad times, when we call on God to help us. We need to pray and thank him for everything he has blessed us with. I am so thankful to him for my wife, Jessica, and my son, Owen. I try to be the husband that God wants me to be, and I want to set a proper example for my son to grow up to be a man of God.

STAY FAITH-DRIVEN AND MOTIVATED. BE PASSIONATE ABOUT EVERYTHING YOU DO.

When he gets older, I will tell my son what I tell any person when their opportunity arises: Stay faith-driven and motivated. Be passionate about everything you do. Work hard and stay humble. Be helpful when you can and love people as Christ loved us. We are here on earth to be iron-willed in doing God's will.

CHAPTER 5

SHAMARKO THOMAS
Destined IV Greatness

@shamarko21ya Bro, I thought I was the only person on this earth who would do 5 workouts in 1 day until I met you. Haha! We have similar careers . . . We know we the best. The Opportunity is on its way!! Just trust God, he won't leave us hangin!! #DIVG Work Hard & Stay Humble.

Syracuse University	Virginia Beach, VA	Safety

Shamarko Thomas lined up near the goal line at Lucas Oil Stadium in Indianapolis. As one of nearly sixty defensive backs invited to the 2013 NFL Scouting Combine, he knew he had to do something to stand out. He set his feet, got down in his stance, and prepared for the 40-yard dash.

Wearing a camouflage-green top and neon-yellow shoes, the announcers marveled at the physicality and fierceness of this 5'9", 213-pound safety from Syracuse University. "If you watch him on tape, he's like a heat-seeking missile to the football," one said. And that's what Shamarko looked like when the gun sounded. He exploded out of his stance, flew down the field, and crossed the finish line in a blazing 4.42 seconds. His impressive time wasn't the only thing that immediately caught the attention of NFL scouts in attendance, though.

At the finish line, his left foot caught the turf. Two strides later, Shamarko went down hard, landing on his chin and shoulder. A lot of guys would've been knocked out by the fall. They would've stayed down. Shamarko popped right back to his feet. Life had already hit him in the toughest possible way, and Shamarko had gotten up. A face-plant into artificial turf, even while running more than eighteen miles per hour, was nothing.

Pittsburgh drafted Shamarko in the fourth round, and he played four seasons for the Steelers. In 2017, he moved north to play for the Buffalo Bills, and in 2018 signed with the Denver Broncos. Life for an NFL player can be filled with uncertainty. Through it all—the good, the bad, and even the *really* bad—Shamarko has held on to his faith. No matter how many times he gets knocked down, he continues to get up again and again.

It was April 18, 2011. My phone vibrated with a text message from my cousin: *Call home immediately.* I was a sophomore at Syracuse University. On the field, things were good. The previous year, I had been selected to the All-Big East All-Freshman Team after starting games at linebacker, corner-back, and safety. Then, this sophomore season, I'd played all thirteen games and had thirty-eight tackles. But off the field, life had been challenging ever since I left home for college.

In July of 2010, my stepfather was killed in a motorcycle accident. I was still deeply hurting over his loss. He hadn't been the greatest of role models, but he was the only father I'd known. Now all I had left was my mother. For most of my life, that's the way it had been. She was my best friend.

So while I didn't know what was so urgent, I called home right away as my cousin had instructed.

My younger brother answered the call and simply said, "Momma's gone."

I went into shock. My mother. My inspiration. My source of love and strength. My ultimate leader. Gone. After my stepfather died, I'd drawn even closer to my mother. Immediately, I thought back to a conversation I'd had with her just a couple days earlier. It was like God had given me the chance to say goodbye to her before he took her home. My mom had called just as I was getting ready to go out for the night. Thankfully, I took the time to speak with her, even though my friends and I were already late, and they kept trying to hurry me along. At the end of the phone call, my mother prophetically said, "If anything ever happens to me, accomplish your dreams and work hard. You are my chosen one. I love you." She was always telling me, "You are my chosen one."

> **"IF ANYTHING EVER HAPPENS TO ME, ACCOMPLISH YOUR DREAMS AND WORK HARD."**

"I love you too," I told her. "I'll talk to you later." Then we left for the party. I never had the chance to speak to her again. She passed away in her sleep from a massive heart attack.

I was now alone at Syracuse, at a loss as to how I could help raise my four younger brothers and sister, who lived back in Virginia Beach and ranged in age from seventeen to five. At twenty years old, I was not only the oldest child, I had just become the patriarch of the family.

My mom had been my everything. She was the hardest-working woman I'd ever known. She'd work at McDonald's, often two jobs, to help support us and our dreams. My coaches often wondered why I worked so hard in the weight room or ran hills and did drills even after practice was over. That was why. My mom never took a break, so I couldn't take a break. I wanted my mom to have a big house, cars, and a good life. Now I couldn't give those things to her.

She had been the one to try and make sure we were in church on Sundays. I believed in God as a kid. At least, I believed there *was* a God. I just didn't want much to do with him. I was always trying to get out of going to church. Sitting still that long wasn't easy for me. I had a lot of energy as a kid, and that sometimes got me in trouble. I used to fight a lot. My friends and I only wanted to hang out. So mostly, the whole church thing felt like a big waste of time.

I went back to Virginia for the funeral. I tried not to cry. I wanted to be strong for my brothers and sister. Speaking at my mother's funeral, I looked around at my amazing support system. They were the only reason I didn't break down. My head coach from Syracuse, Doug Marrone, was there. The defensive coordinator and graduate assistant had also come down from New York. My high school football coach sat in the audience; so did our school police officer, Adam Bernstein, and guidance counselor, Leslie Allard.

Back in high school, I'd spent a lot of time in the principal's office talking with Miss Leslie. She was a tremendous help to me. When I was a freshman at Ocean Lakes High, I was involved with the wrong kind of people and didn't care about my grades. Thanks to Miss Leslie and my mom, I got on the right path. I started working hard on the football field and in the classroom. I made the honor roll my junior and senior years. Not only did Miss Leslie work with me to keep up my grades, she guided me throughout the recruiting process—helping me prepare to take the SAT, speak with scouts, and analyze college scholarship offers. In fact, she's the only reason I went to college. Growing up, I thought college was just something you saw on television. To this day, I still stay in touch with Miss Leslie.

My journey to Syracuse had not been an easy one. Now, without my parents, it was even harder. My grandmother and I went to the courthouse to claim dual custody of my brothers and sister. I knew the only way we would make it was with Grandma's help. I had about two weeks to figure out a future that was no longer just mine—it would affect five other young people. I could stay in Virginia Beach and get a job, or I could go back to college for finals.

Shamarko (21) tackling Nate Nord while at Syracuse
>> Rich Barnes/Icon SMI CCM/Newscom

I was lost. I was mad at my circumstances and mad at God. I thought my life was over. I felt like God didn't love me. It was the most painful feeling in the world. I couldn't understand how the Lord could allow my family to lose both parents. How could I raise five siblings while going to college and making no money? I remember saying to God, *Lord, you gave me the gift of football talent so that I could take care of my mom. You already took my dad. My mom was who I lived for! Why would you do this to me?*

My grandma agreed to take care of my brothers and sister. Miss Leslie asked me, "What would your mom want you to do?" I knew the answer. I chose to stay in school. I threw myself into my workouts, but I was also partying hard to try and dull my pain. I wasn't making great decisions, but God stuck with me. My Christian teammates were there for me as well. That's when I first became interested in God on my own. But I still had my questions, like, *Can I believe in God after everything I've been through?* I didn't know. But by his grace, I was drafted by the Pittsburgh Steelers in the fourth round of the 2013 NFL Draft. Maybe my mother's words could come true. I'd be her chosen one . . . Destined IV Greatness.

GOD'S **SOLDIER**

I define myself as God's soldier. My favorite Scripture verse reflects what I've been through in my life. Isaiah 54:17 states, "No weapon forged against you will prevail, and you will refute every tongue that accuses you. This is the heritage of the servants of the Lord, and this is their vindication from me." God was always there for me, protecting me—even in the times I didn't seek him out. He has helped me prevail every time I've felt attacked by life. Now I'm a God-lover and a God-seeker!

HALL OF FAME MENTOR

When I was drafted, the Steelers already had a strong safety. Actually, they had one of the best players to ever play the position, Troy Polamalu. Troy was an eight-time Pro Bowler, six-time All-Pro, and two-time Super Bowl champion. He even won the NFL Defensive Player of the Year Award for his 2010 season. The Black and Gold knew that Troy was nearing retirement. Pittsburgh would need to replace him in the lineup soon. Some veterans can be bitter when the end of their career approaches, but Troy was classy. He took me under his wing and began teaching me the finer points of the game.

I wanted to learn everything I could from him. One night I sent Troy a text message: *I want to be great in this game.* He took his time replying, but eventually texted back: *What is your definition of greatness?* I answered: *Working hard and dedicating myself to the game of football.* Again, I didn't get a response right away. Finally, Troy replied, and his definition of greatness was nowhere near mine: *Greatness comes by putting God first in your life and by building a foundation for your family.* When a superstar like Troy explained greatness by starting with God first, it finally dawned on me. Life is bigger than football.

Troy and I started training together. It was just another example of Troy's extraordinary character. Here I was, working to one day take his job, and he's doing everything to make me better. Our training sessions were much more than physical workouts. I also saw how spiritually focused Troy was. Football was only a small part of his life. Some people act one way in public and are completely different in private. Troy wasn't like that. He was consistent. His walk with the Lord didn't change. After witnessing Troy's example, I made the decision to truly accept Christ as my Savior. I put my trust in God's Word and placed my life in God's hands because of the witness of my mentor, Troy Polamalu.

My journey to success wasn't easy. No journey worth taking is. Whether it's sports, school, or the journey of life—you won't find any shortcuts. If somebody tells you differently, it's a lie. The Lord knows I wanted to be the starting safety for the Steelers after Troy left. That would have been *my* perfect plan. It just didn't work out that way. But as Christians, we must follow *God's plans* for our lives. Through uncertainty, disappointment, and the enemy's schemes to get me to give up on my dream, I still stand firm. I encourage you to do the same. Know that all you need to have is a faith in God that you place first in your life, and a solid work ethic to follow. God may test your faith like he did mine. But now that I live for Christ, I know that every step I take, God's taking a step with me. And with God standing beside me, I AM truly Destined IV Greatness.

Shamarko prepares himself for a game against the Philadelphia Eagles

>> Chris Szagola/AP/Shutterstock

CHAPTER 6

MATTHEW SLATER
The Improbable Journey

Man, you have no social media. Haha. But you have like 2 Super Rings and 100 Pro Bowls. Lol. I'll take those any day! We always competing against each other, but you will always be my brother in Christ!! #GOAT

UCLA	Orange, CA	Wide Receiver/Special Teams

What do you think the odds would be of a NFL team drafting a player who never started a single game in college? Would those odds change if this player was a wide receiver who made NO receptions during his college career? That's right—*zero, zip, zilch, nil, nada!* Now what if you found out this player also played defensive back in college and had no interceptions. Would you think this athlete had an outstanding NFL career ahead of him?

Well, as unlikely as it seems, the New England Patriots *did* pick that player in the fifth round of the 2008 NFL Draft, and Matthew Slater *has* gone on to excel in the NFL. While Matthew was never an offensive or defensive standout during his four years at UCLA, he was an excellent special teams player. Matthew specialized in making big hits on kick coverage. And when he went back to return a kick, he was one of the nation's best.

During his senior year, Matthew led the Pac-10 Conference in kickoff yardage and returned three kickoffs for touchdowns! The Patriots drafted this special teams ace to head up an important phase of the game. Matthew rose to the challenge of playing for one of the most successful and demanding organizations in the league, being selected to the Pro Bowl seven times and earning first-team All-Pro honors in 2011, 2012, 2014, and 2016. He also helped the Patriots win two Super Bowls.

Matthew and Tom Brady hug after winning Super Bowl XLIX

≫ David J. Phillip/AP/Shutterstock

Matthew is a perfect example of finding an area where you're gifted and then working as hard as you can to become the best. His example of following Christ is no different.

My story begins just outside of Los Angeles, California. My father is NFL Hall of Famer Jackie Slater. He played twenty seasons for the Rams and is considered one of the greatest offensive tackles the league has ever seen. If you never watched him play, check out his highlights on YouTube. A lot of times you could've driven a truck through the space my dad's blocks created.

As much as my dad loved football, he loves God more. I regularly went to church with my parents and learned about God's Word. My parents didn't just go to church—they lived out their faith. They also showed me and my brother, David, what a healthy and loving marriage looked like. In fact, they've been married for more than forty years.

My parents were intentional about everything, even making sure we truly understood the gospel. When I was about seven years old, my dad sat me down for a very important talk. He opened his Bible and explained who Christ was, why he came to earth as a man, how he sacrificed himself on the cross for my sins, and God's plan of salvation. I saw the faith my dad had. I knew God loved me. That night I gave my life to Christ and secured my eternal home in heaven.

Matthew as a child, with his dad

›› Photo courtesy of Matthew Slater

Over the years, my faith grew as my understanding of the Scriptures deepened. Attending a Christian school helped me learn more about God. Throughout middle and high school, I was mainly around people who shared my beliefs. That changed in college.

In my last two years in high school, I started to stand out on the football field. I caught more than sixty passes for over 1,000 yards and scored seven touchdowns. I was also one of the fastest athletes in the state of California, clocking 10.62 seconds in the 100 meters. USC offered me a track scholarship. But UCLA gave me a full-ride to play football. I chose to attend UCLA. The Bruins' campus in Los Angeles was filled with students from different faiths and different beliefs. It was also filled with temptations. More than any other time in my life, I strayed from my faith and started to question my beliefs in college.

Part of it was being around more than 40,000 students, most of whom didn't share my faith in God. But many of my doubts came from my frustrations on the football field. I had turf toe during my freshman year and suffered through a stress fracture in my leg as a sophomore. It seemed like I could never get on the field. I thought to myself, *I've lived my life to honor God, so why aren't things working out?* Looking back, I was being immature. I was treating God like a heavenly ATM machine. I figured if I put "money" into my spiritual bank account, I should get all that back . . . with interest.

I COULDN'T BOAST ABOUT ANYTHING I'D DONE . . . GOD'S GRACE HAD PROVIDED FOR ME.

But God didn't hold that against me. He can handle our doubts, and he showed himself in my life big-time.

During the next two years at UCLA, I made a name for myself on special teams. Kickoffs and kick coverage allowed me to use my speed and elusiveness on the field. When the Patriots drafted me, I knew it could only be because of God. Based on my college stats, I shouldn't have been given the opportunity. I couldn't boast about anything I'd done. God was developing me. His grace had provided for me. Seeing God work that way and open that door helped me become secure in my faith once again.

And God has continued to show his faithfulness. There are so many emotional, physical, and mental challenges we all have to overcome every week. For me, my faith in God has helped me to be totally dependent upon him, because there is so much in my life I can't control. My career has been unique in the way it happened, and I can see the way the Lord has worked in mighty ways to bring me through different circumstances.

I've also seen God bring the Patriots and our city through difficult circumstances. When terrorists detonated two bombs at the 2013 Boston Marathon, our city was in shock. So was our team. Many of the Patriots had gathered at Gillette Stadium for off-season workouts that morning. When we heard the news reports, Coach Bill Belichick asked me to talk to the team and offer a prayer.

Being a Christian is the most important thing in my life. My teammates and coaches know that. They also know that I'm not going to beat them over the head with a Bible. I want to show God's love through my actions.

Being a Christian means I am a person who received God's grace when I didn't deserve it. Because of that, I'm going to do everything I can to be an imitator and follower of Jesus Christ. It's a lifestyle. It's the life that God's Word calls us to accept and embrace. And even though I am committed to that life, I'm not perfect. I fail, as we all do, but I continue to strive for the standard that Christ set.

Inviting Christ into my heart as a seven-year-old was the most important decision I ever made. If you don't have a personal relationship with God, I strongly encourage you to investigate Jesus. You may have questions about who he is and what he has done for you. Those are great

Matthew (center) leading prayer with players from the Patriots and the Bills after a game
>> Elise Amendola/AP/Shutterstock

questions to ask. Find a friend, teacher, relative, or coach who knows Christ. Go to church and talk to a pastor, or pick up a Bible. It's not too late, and the answers are there. God wants to be a part of your life.

ALL **FOR** GOOD

My favorite verse is Romans 8:28: "And we know that in all things God works for the good of those who love him, who have been called according to his purpose." When I was going through a number of obstacles and challenges during college, my father shared this verse with me. It reminds me that no matter what is happening in my life, God is in control. It also tells me that life isn't always about me and my personal good. Sometimes it's about the greater good God is working toward. God refines all of us during our lifetimes, and Romans 8:28 reassures me that he has it all under his control, so I don't need to worry.

Having God at the center of my life has helped me see the importance of every person on the team. In 1 Corinthians 12, the apostle Paul describes how God's people work together as one body with many parts. It's that way on a football team too. Every role on a team is critical to the team's success. Some positions get more fanfare and media attention than other positions, but the success of a team depends on all players doing their job. When I first went to college, I was looking for personal glory. But as I allowed the Lord to use my talents for his glory, I saw how playing special teams was something I was totally suited for. That's how God blessed me—and he'll do the same for you.

I'm so thankful that God used the game of football to teach me about dependency on him. My story isn't over, but I've already seen God do more than I thought possible. In 2017, I won the prestigious Athletes in Action Bart Starr Award, which is given annually to the player who best exemplifies outstanding character and leadership in the home, on the field, and in the community. My dad won this same award in 1996, making us the first father-son duo to be honored with that award. Sometimes I'm still in awe that this award and the others I've been given came to a player who never started a single college game. I just played the role that I was assigned to the best of my ability. I'm honored to be a Super Bowl champion, but my favorite honor is to be a child of God. This is how my improbable journey started, and I know it's far from finished.

> **I'M HONORED TO BE A SUPER BOWL CHAMPION, BUT MY FAVORITE HONOR IS TO BE A CHILD OF GOD.**

Matthew and teammate Julian Edelman visiting fans at the Children's Hospital Boston

» Darren McCollester/WireImage for Children's Hospital Boston/Getty Images

CHAPTER 7

TYSON ALUALU
God First

@Talualu93 aka MAUI. Haha, naw I'm playin bro! You been an absolute beast in the league for a while now. Former 1st round pick and everything! Let's make the rest of our careers GREAT bro! Just like we vowed to do in Israel.

University of California, Berkeley	Honolulu, HI	Defensive End

When Tyson Alualu was chosen as the tenth overall pick in the first round of the 2010 NFL Draft, he had just one reaction: to praise God. "I never thought it would be like this," Tyson said to a newspaper in Hawaii. "I give the glory to God. Nobody thought I would be the tenth pick, it's crazy!"

That first season in Jacksonville, he was named to the NFL's 2010 All-Rookie Team. During his seven seasons with the Jaguars, the defensive tackle and defensive end recorded 17.5 sacks. His versatility on the line made him a perfect signing by the Pittsburgh Steelers in 2017. Heading into the 2018 season, Tyson will feel the breeze of the Terrible Towel-waving Pittsburgh fans as he chases down quarterbacks in the opponent's backfield.

Through his gridiron exploits and his godly example, Tyson has proven to be a terror on the field and a warrior for Christ.

As a boy, I pictured myself as a future NFL running back. My inspiration was my uncle Tupu, who had been a running back at the University of Hawaii before an injury ended his career.

In Pop Warner football, I dominated the game as a running back, often scoring two or three touchdowns to lead my team to victory. As fun as the games were with the Palama Scorpions, the after-game potluck was even better! Food is a central part of Polynesian culture. At these meals, coaches, teammates, and their parents would praise me for the way I played. I wished those meals would go on forever. Because after the festivities came something I dreaded—the car ride home with my father. Like many hyper-driven sports parents, my dad would lecture me on what I could've done better. I only wanted my father's love, but instead I got his wrath. He never seemed satisfied, regardless of how well I played. Here I was, the hero of the game, and I'd spend the car ride home with tears streaming down my face.

I ONLY WANTED MY FATHER'S LOVE, BUT INSTEAD I GOT HIS WRATH.

I loved my dad, but I also feared him. Growing up, I saw him do drugs, get into fights, and carry weapons. I was raised in Honolulu, Hawaii, in an affordable housing project known as Kuhio Park Terrace. We were a tight-knit family. When I tell people that I was one of nine children—seven girls and two boys—they think that sounds like a lot. But with so many cousins running around our home, I actually had a much bigger family than that. Our house was always full of people and full of love.

STRENGTH **FROM** ABOVE

Growing up, my favorite Bible verse was Philippians 4:13 (NKJV): "I can do all things through Christ who strengthens me." This verse gave me strength in times of challenge. More recently, during my years in the NFL, I often quote 2 Timothy 1:7 (NKJV): "For God has not given us a spirit of fear, but of power and of love and of a sound mind." I recite this verse to myself before games. It reminds me to trust God and the abilities he has given me. He gave me my desire and passion for the game of football. To me, playing football is an act of worship where I use my talents to glorify God.

Church meant a lot to my family. The entire Alualu *ohana*, including my father, went to church each Sunday. But we didn't live like it from Monday to Saturday. I had knowledge of the Bible and of Jesus and God, but that knowledge was in my head and not in my heart.

That changed the last time my dad got out of prison. As a kid, my dad was incarcerated at different periods for a variety of drug charges, gang activities, and violence. When I was seven years old, God changed my father's life. He accepted Christ as his Savior and was a different person when he came out of prison. My parents began to live their faith in a genuine way. For the first time, I began to see God was real. At this time, my dad coined our family motto: God First.

During my middle school years, I made the decision to ask Christ to be the Lord of my life. A speaker at church asked, "If you died this morning, would you go to heaven?" I knew that I wouldn't, so I walked up to the altar and prayed to God to save me. I felt renewed, different. This wasn't the end of my troubles. If you hang out with the wrong crowd, you will make mistakes, and there were plenty of ways to get into trouble where I grew up. But when you confess your sins to God, like I did many times, he forgives you.

In high school, I grew in my faith and physically grew in size. My dreams of playing in the NFL remained, but I'd given up on being a running back. There just aren't many 6'3", 310-pound running backs in the league. But my size and strength made me a perfect defensive end. I was a two-time all-state selection by the *Honolulu Star Bulletin*. By the time I graduated, I was ranked as the second-best player in Hawaii.

I accepted a scholarship to play football at the University of California, Berkeley. I'd never been off the island of Hawaii, but the Bears had one of the top programs in the country. I knew playing in the Pac-10 would give me the opportunity to make the next step toward the NFL and provide for my family.

Yes, *my* family.

Tyson with his wife and still-growing family while playing for the University of California
>> Photo courtesy of Tyson Alualu

During my senior year of high school, my girlfriend, Desiré, who is now my wife, became pregnant with our first child. There was never any doubt in my mind about keeping the baby or getting married. Even though I was only eighteen years old, I stepped up to the responsibility. I enrolled in summer school at

UC Berkeley. But before the regular semester started, I returned home and married Desiré two months before she gave birth.

We flew back to California as a family to begin our lives together. I had a wife, a child, and was entering a highly academic college and a competitive football program. It was only through the grace of God and his forgiveness and love that I made it.

At times, I felt so homesick. I was away from everything and everyone I knew. I wanted to leave California and go home to Hawaii. During those times, Desiré would say we needed to pray about God's direction for our lives. We had to put God first. It was then that the proverbial light came on, and I started to mature even more in my faith.

On the football field, I played in all thirteen games during my first season with the Bears. God blessed me with good health. I started in my next thirty-nine games at Cal, earning first-team All-Pac-10 honors as a senior. Then at the 2010 Senior Bowl, my draft stock rose even higher. I finished the game with a sack, forced fumble, and fumble recovery.

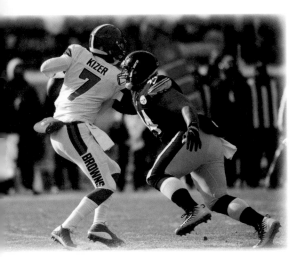

Tyson (right), seconds before sacking quarterback DeShone Kizer during a 2017 game against the Cleveland Browns

>> Jason Pohuski/CSM/Shutterstock

Being drafted tenth overall by Jacksonville surprised some experts. Before the season started, I signed a five-year deal with the Jaguars that gave my growing family financial security. God had provided!

I played seven years in Jacksonville. Then, in 2017, the Pittsburgh Steelers signed me. It was great going to a team with a perennial winning record. With Ben Roethlisberger at quarterback, Pittsburgh was almost always in the playoffs—something I hadn't experienced with the Jaguars. Even before I joined the team, I respected Ben as a player and a Christian.

To me, being a Christian means having a personal relationship with Jesus Christ and being real and genuine in everything about your faith. I know that as a Christian I represent Jesus. Everything I do at home, at practice, or on the field should reflect who Jesus is. As believers, we need to take on Christ's likeness and show the world the love that he shows to us.

Every day, I thank God for placing the right people in my life. My family is such an inspiration to me. My father transformed from being a man I once feared—a violent prisoner and felon—to a man of God who is now the pastor of the Solid Rock Fellowship

Tyson with his hometown "support team"

➤ Photo courtesy of Tyson Alualu

Assembly of God in Honolulu. I am also the product of a praying woman, my mother. And of course my wife, Desiré, is my number one supporter in life as well as in football. As a father myself, I dearly love our five children: sons Tyreé, Tydes, Tyten, and Jaxx, and our daughter, Dereon. I know I would not have this support team behind me if I didn't put God First!

CHAPTER 8

BEN ROETHLISBERGER

Get Back Up

Come on, Big Ben, no social media. Haha. Naw . . .
you Mr. Do It All. Man, you got the juice!! You're a
role model to more people than you can imagine!
Continue to give God the glory in all you do. You
a Hall of Famer in my eyes! #Legend #GOATstatus
#Steelernation

University of Miami, Ohio	Lima, OH	Quarterback

Ben Roethlisberger has plenty of football left in the tank. But when he concludes his career, it's very likely that this Pittsburgh Steelers quarterback will be elected into the Pro Football Hall of Fame. Ben ranks among the top ten quarterbacks all-time in career passing yards, passing touchdowns, passer rating, and fourth-quarter comebacks. Heading into the 2018 season, he's been selected to the Pro Bowl six times, has been the AFC Offensive Player of the Week fourteen times, and was the 2004 NFL Offensive Rookie of the Year. The highlights Ben has created with his right arm are too numerous to count. But the play Ben may be remembered for most came from using his legs.

It was the 2006 AFC divisional playoff game between Pittsburgh and Indianapolis. The Black and Gold's star running back, Jerome Bettis, had announced it would be his last season. The Super Bowl would be played in Detroit, Michigan, which happened to be the hometown of "The Bus," as Bettis was called. The Steelers led the Colts 21–18 with 1:20 left in the game. Pittsburgh had moved the ball to the Colts' 2-yard line. Now was the time to ride The Bus into the end zone and ice the victory. Ben took the snap and handed the ball to Bettis—no surprise there. The surprise came when Colts linebacker Gary Brackett shot into the hole, lowered his helmet, made direct contact with the football, and forced the normally sure-handed Bettis to fumble. The ball flew into the air, bounced on the ground, and was scooped up by Colts defensive back Nick Harper. The speedy Harper zoomed down the field. Only one player, Ben Roethlisberger, stood between him and a Colts touchdown. Ben backpedaled furiously, hoping to slow down Harper and allow his Steeler teammates to catch up. Harper juked to his right and cut left, trying to fly past the quarterback. Off balance, Ben dove sideways, stretched out his 6'5"

Ben with the Steelers' Super Bowl XLII trophy
>> Mark Humphrey/AP/Shutterstock

frame to maximum reach, and brought down Harper on the 42-yard line. It was literally a Super Bowl-ride-saving tackle. The Steelers went on to win the divisional game, the AFC Championship game, and then the Super Bowl!

Ben may not be the nimblest athlete to play quarterback, but nobody wants to win more or is tougher than the 240-pounder from Findlay, Ohio. He's been sacked more than 475 times and knocked down thousands more. The number of injuries he has sustained over his career are as numerous as they are serious. But Ben finds a way to keep pushing on and playing through. A torn meniscus in his left knee in 2016 resulted in only two missed games. In 2015, he missed four games with sprained ligaments in his knee. In 2012, a sprained throwing shoulder and dislocated rib caused two missed games, but he played through a badly sprained ankle. A fractured hand in 2011 led to just one missed game. In 2010, Ben missed four games with a broken foot, sprained ankle, and dislocated shoulder. His list of injuries could go on and on. Many players would've been out for the season after sustaining similar injuries, but not Ben. Through his faith and tenacity, he just gets back up!

———————

One of my favorite poems is called "Don't Quit" by John Greenleaf Whittier. The last few lines really resonate with me:

> *Success is failure turned inside out—*
> *The silver tint of the clouds of doubt,*
> *And you never can tell just how close you are,*
> *It may be near when it seems so far;*
> *So stick to the fight when you're hardest hit—*
> *It's when things seem worst that you must not quit.*

I've taken devastating blows on the football field and in life. When I was eight, my mother was killed in a car accident. My dad later married a wonderful woman named Brenda, who I call Mom, but the pain remained. My grandfather, Ken, passed away in 2006, before he ever got to see me play for the Steelers. I'd been very close to my grandfather, and his death was another difficult punch to take. Then, in 2007, my college coach from Miami University (Ohio), Terry Hoeppner, died of brain cancer. Coach Hoeppner was like a second father to me. The loss of these three very important mentors knocked me down.

LIFTED **UP**

My favorite Bible verse ties into the theme of getting back up. Psalm 37:24 says, "Though he may stumble, he will not fall, for the Lord upholds him with his hand." This verse speaks volumes for life as well as for football. We all stumble and fall short of the glory of God. We all make mistakes, and we all sin. In football, I may throw interceptions and lose games. All these things happen because we are so far from perfect. But even though we stumble sometimes, we never fall, because God lifts us up. He always forgives us and always loves us.

The losses I'd experienced caused me to have questions and to feel anger and doubt. But though I was mad at God, I didn't stay that way. That's because my dad and stepmom raised me and my sister, Carlee, in the church, and I grew up in a great family—parents, grandparents, aunts, and uncles. The combination of never missing church and the Christian examples in my family gave me a great foundation of faith. And it was my faith in God that helped me get back up. Instead of dwelling on my sorrow at the loss of my mom, grandfather, and Coach Hoeppner, I turned their lives into my motivation. I play the game for them. And I know they have the best seats in the house every Sunday!

I'm so glad that my dad instilled Christian values in me at an early age. I remember wanting to go to prom my junior year of high school. The dance was held on a Saturday night. My dad said it was okay to go, but I had to be in church on Sunday. Looking back, that commitment to God and to attending church got me motivated to be the best I can be for Jesus Christ. Since getting married in 2011, my wife and I are teaching those same values to our children. My upbringing shaped me into the man and father I am today.

Ben as a child

>> Photo courtesy of Ben Roethlisberger

Much of what people see of me is on the football field. No one wants to win more than I do. But I leave the outcome of the game in the Lord's hands. All I can do is go onto the field and be the best I can be to live up to his plan. I take the approach that I'm going to give it everything I have and leave it all out there. I want to glorify God, my teammates, and my loved ones in every action and every play of every game. My desire is that the Lord is proud of me and would say, "Great job, you gave it your all today."

In my early years in the NFL, I wrote "PFJ" on my cleats before I took the field. It was my way of telling the world I was "Playing for Jesus." But I don't just play for Jesus; I live for him as well. I'm committed to being a Christian—a believer in Jesus Christ, a believer in God, and a believer in the Bible. I believe that God is the Almighty who created everything, holds everything in his hands, and knows our every thought and emotion.

And I confess that Jesus came to earth and died for our sins so that we can be with him someday in heaven.

I'm blessed to be able to throw a football for a living, but that doesn't make me any better than anyone else in the Lord's eyes. I'm a sinner, just like everyone. I believe he has a plan for all of us, one that includes forgiveness and a second chance at living the life he wants us to have. We need to live by his plan—not our own plan—because he is a perfect and awesome God.

We show our love to God by following his commands. In my experience, when you show your love to God, he will show you more love than you know what to do with. That love

Ben, giving his all on the field
>> Winslow Townson/AP/Shutterstock

will reveal itself in whatever you choose to do in life. If you rely on God, you will be the best you can be with the talent he has gifted you.

God has blessed me with a multitude of honors. Most people think my greatest achievements were winning Super Bowl XL and Super Bowl XLIII.

But my greatest honor is to be called a follower of Jesus Christ. I encourage you to focus on the same. Love Jesus with all your heart. Commit your life to him. When you fully and truly commit to God and are serious about it, you will experience a joy and a pleasure in life, in sports, and in relationships that you've never been able to experience before. And when life knocks you down, you'll find a strength and power that will help you get back up!

MY GREATEST HONOR IS TO BE CALLED A FOLLOWER OF JESUS CHRIST.

CHAPTER 9

WESLEY WOODYARD

A Leader Prays

@**WoodDro52** aka "Wood," my big bro in the league. Showed me the ropes . . . Undrafted and just an all-around baller. Always overlooked smh, but you get the job done EZ!! Even though you went to UK (University of Kentucky) smh haha! #Lumberjack #WPMOY I'm literally following in your footsteps bro! Keep leading!!

University of Kentucky	LaGrange, GA	Linebacker

One of the all-time greatest football coaches, Vince Lombardi, once said, "Leaders are made, they are not born. They are made by hard effort, which is the price which all of us must pay to achieve any goal that is worthwhile."

Coach Lombardi led the Green Bay Packers through much of the 1960s and won the first two Super Bowls, so he never met Wesley Woodyard. Yet his words perfectly describe the standout Tennessee Titans linebacker.

Wesley is a leader by anyone's definition. He's honest, positive, committed, a good communicator, and he lives by his convictions. As he enters his eleventh NFL season—six years with the Denver Broncos and four with the Titans—Wesley has been nominated four times for the Walter Payton Man of the Year Award, the NFL's highest honor for a player who best exemplifies volunteer and charitable work along with excellence on the field. That's impressive enough, but consider this: he's been named a team captain during all ten of his NFL seasons. In fact, if you go back to his high school days in Georgia and his college career at the University of Kentucky, Wesley has been named a team captain for fifteen consecutive seasons and counting!

The Titans recently extended his contract, and he had his best season as a pro in 2017. Wesley started all sixteen games, recording a career-high 124 tackles. He also had five pass deflections and five sacks. Wesley's contributions on and off the field make him a NFL great. Much of his career can be credited to hard work and a winning attitude. But when Wesley looks at his years in the league, he sees them as an answer to a lot of prayers.

———————

I'm undersized for a linebacker—I've been hearing that for most of my life. But ever since I stepped onto a football field, I've been proving critics wrong. Being six feet tall and 230 pounds, I know there are bigger athletes and harder hitters at the position. But what can't be measured is my ability to read plays and my nose for the ball.

I grew up in Georgia. My dad was a hard worker, and my mom owned a daycare and raised me and my brothers in the church. Some of my favorite memories are having thirty people crammed into the house for Sunday dinners. The smell of food and a feeling of love were everywhere. Family was important to me. In fact, my cousin, Derrick, was a huge part of my life. He instilled a lot of very important values in me that helped me become the person I am today.

I played varsity football for all the four years I attended LaGrange High School. For two of those seasons, I was an outside linebacker, earning Class AAA Defensive Player of the Year and being named first-team all-state as a senior. After winning two state championships in high school, I decided to play football at the University of Kentucky.

At first, the Wildcats tried to make me a strong safety. But halfway into my freshman season, I was moved to inside linebacker. Immediately, I started impacting the game. I was selected to the Freshman All-Southeastern Conference Team. From there, I had one hundred tackles or more in the next three seasons—even leading the SEC in tackles as a junior and senior. On the field, I was an all-SEC player for two consecutive seasons. Off the field, I was a standout with my academics. I'd been projected as an early second-round pick in the 2008 NFL Draft. But God humbled me.

Wesley (in blue) tackling Kent State's Eugene Jarvis while at the University of Kentucky
>> Andy Lions/Getty Images

After seven rounds, I didn't get a call from any NFL teams. Twenty-seven linebackers were selected—I wasn't one of them. Two days after the draft, the Denver Broncos called and signed me to a three-year deal. But that didn't take away the sting of going undrafted. I felt like the NFL had rejected me. Going undrafted makes some guys play with a chip on their shoulder, and that's the way I reacted. I rededicated myself to the game of football. My focus became sharper and my love of the sport became stronger. I'd thought I was special in the game of football when I was in college, but my mindset changed when I became the lowest man on the totem pole after going undrafted.

I threw all my efforts into proving that I belonged in the NFL. I played in the Broncos season opener and made my first start at linebacker a couple months later. I also excelled on special teams, where I was named team captain.

After three years in the league, I was a consistent special teams performer and splitting time at linebacker. From the outside, it probably looked like I'd arrived. But inside, I found myself at a dark place in my spiritual walk. At a young age, I had given my life to the Lord. My mother was a Southern Baptist Sunday school teacher, so I'd found myself in church on Sundays from the early morning until evening. In 2011, I was still attending church in Denver, but I'd pretty much stopped praying and reading my Bible. I knew I'd drifted away from the intimate relationship that I'd long enjoyed with my Savior.

It was around that time that God brought Veronica into my life. She was a Christian and an answer to my prayers. We met in Miami in the off season. We started dating and got married. Shortly thereafter, I rededicated my life to Christ after attending a Christian conference and feeling convicted. I knew I couldn't lead my family in godly ways until I totally dedicated myself to God. I credit God for leading Veronica and me to each other and for the renewal I experienced in my relationship with the Lord.

> **FROM THE OUTSIDE, IT PROBABLY LOOKED LIKE I'D ARRIVED. BUT INSIDE, I FOUND MYSELF AT A DARK PLACE.**

RISE **UP**

One of my favorite Bible verses is Proverbs 24:16: "For though the righteous fall seven times, they rise again, but the wicked stumble when calamity strikes." That verse represents my football life. As the smallest guy at my position, no one thought I had a chance to succeed. But with God's help, I always have and always will get back up every time I fall. You can't succeed if you don't get back up and try. God chose to use me as an example to other people. We all will encounter trials in life, but I choose to persevere and not to give up.

In 2011, I had my best year to date as a pro. The Broncos had given me a one-year contract, and I made nearly one hundred tackles that season. The 2012 season went even better. I had 117 tackles, five-and-a-half sacks, and three interceptions. I wasn't a star coming into the NFL, but those statistics put me among the league's best.

When people ask me how I achieved my goals, I tell them there's nothing special about me. God's blessing is the reason I even got a chance in the league. If you work hard, focus, dedicate yourself, and pray, you can overcome the difficult times in life.

As football players, we always tell each other not to worry about the things we can't control. It's natural for an athlete to worry about making the team or botching a play. We harshly critique our own performance. But instead of worrying, we just need to seek God. Jesus said to "seek first his kingdom and his righteousness, and all these things will be given to you as well. Therefore do not worry about tomorrow, for tomorrow will worry about itself. Each day has enough trouble of its own" (Matthew 6:33–34). If you put all your trust in the Lord, you are going to be fine.

Wesley (59) tackling Jacoby Brissett, stopping a
Colts' drive near the end of the fourth quarter

》》 AP/Shutterstock

This doesn't only apply to football. If you work for a company and you always worry about being fired tomorrow, you won't give your best effort today. Leave that worry with God. Pray and turn your fears and concerns over to him. If you happen to lose your job, or get cut by your team, I encourage you to look at it as God expanding his kingdom into another area. He will use your witness to change the lives of others in another job setting or on another team. When unexpected difficulties come up, look at them as God moving you toward something better or away from something negative.

No matter where God puts you, make it your goal to be a shining light for him. That's what I try to do. NFL players have a tremendous platform to show people the love of God. Of course, that platform allows people to clearly see our mistakes as well. That's the beautiful thing about God. He doesn't call perfect people to follow him. He calls sinners like me! His kingdom is for everyone who has a heart open to accepting Jesus as their Savior. He loves you no matter what you've done in your life, no matter your race, color, wealth, or any other factor. There is nothing you can do, either bad or good, that will make God love you more or less than he already does. He will always love you the same.

GOD DOESN'T CALL PERFECT PEOPLE TO FOLLOW HIM.

And once we put our trust in Jesus as our Savior, we become ambassadors for God. Every day as a football player, I get the opportunity to show people that God's will is the only reason I get to live out my childhood dreams. I don't deserve the blessings he has given to me, or the chance to be living the dream of so many young boys who want to play in the NFL. However, since he has allowed me to do this, I will give him the credit and praise him every day of my life! That's what a true leader does—he prays, follows God, and doesn't take the credit for himself.

CHAPTER 10

DON CAREY

God Has a Plan

@DonCarey Man you taught me a lot in Israel bro.
It's definitely something I will never forget! Keep
ballin on the field! I just tryin to be like u when I
grow up! Haha #doncareyspeaks #DC3says #WOC

Norfolk State University	Grand Rapids, MI	Safety

If you ran into Don Carey III on the street, you'd never guess he's a professional football player. At 5'11" and 208 pounds, he's not a hulking behemoth. In fact, when people discover that he's played ten seasons, they often ask, "How did you make it to the NFL?"

Don has the perfect answer. It comes down to Jesus. Don knows he's older, slower, and less talented than most of the guys he plays against. But he also knows his work ethic and faith make up for any limitations. He's been hailed as one of the best special teams players in the league, leading the NFL in solo special team tackles in 2015 and 2016. His fearlessness on the field and for Christ inspires teammates and fans.

I almost didn't make it this far in life. Growing up in Grand Rapids, Michigan, I was abandoned by my father, bullied, poor, and lonely. I used to write poems about wanting to die because of the gaping hole left in my heart from my father not being in my life. It was a horrible feeling that no child should have to grow up with.

My father walked out on our family when I was five years old. He wasn't much of a father to us before that. He was in and out of prison more times than I can remember. But I still looked up to him. He was a legend on playground basketball courts. He never went to college, but he was still offered an NBA tryout. He skipped it, just like he skipped out on our family, leaving my mom to raise my three sisters and me on her own.

To say money was tight would be an understatement. Mom worked hard to support our family, but clothes had to be shared among all of us. That's right—my older sister passed down her clothes to me. Bullies made me their target, and I was laughed at because I once wore the same pair of shoes for two straight years and rarely got new clothes.

Although my dad walked out on us, he didn't go far. He moved into a neighborhood near my school. His house was located down the street from our babysitter's. I would look out the door and see other children playing, working, and laughing with their fathers. But my dad wasn't there for me. I often wondered, *What is wrong with me that my dad doesn't want me?*

Loneliness began to eat away at me. I continued writing poetry to express my feelings about wanting to end my life. When I was only nine, a teacher saw one of the poems I was writing and talked to my mom. I felt worthless, but my mom reminded me of my value.

Eventually, the rejection from my father turned into hate. I hated my father for not being there. I hated wearing my sister's clothes. I hated not having a new pair of shoes. I hated that my mother had to suffer so much to provide for us. Most of all, I hated what my father had done to our family.

Although God wasn't part of my life, I can look back and see his grace at work. I was able to overcome my hatred and use the emotional energy for a positive purpose. I worked hard in the classroom and become a top student. My drive extended onto the high school football field, where, even though I was never the best player, I was always a productive player.

> **I OFTEN WONDERED, WHAT IS WRONG WITH ME THAT MY DAD DOESN'T WANT ME?**

Following high school, no major colleges came calling, so I attended Norfolk State University. I saw more playing time than any other freshman, making sixty-two tackles as a safety. During the next year, I split time between safety and cornerback. By my junior year, I started at cornerback. I was also the recipient of the Spartans Army Strong Award, which is given to the football player who best demonstrates community service and achievement on the field and in the classroom.

Through a lot of hard work, I turned myself from a relatively undersized player into an NFL prospect. My efforts were rewarded in 2009 when the Cleveland Browns drafted me in the sixth round.

JOURNEY TOWARD GOD

Heading into training camp, I signed a four-year deal with Cleveland. Throughout camp, I competed with the other cornerbacks for a position on the team. Unfortunately, a shoulder injury led the Browns to cut me before the preseason even started. A day later, however, the Jacksonville Jaguars claimed me off waivers. They placed me on injured reserve, so I didn't step onto an NFL field until 2010. That year, I started ten games, made my first interception, and recorded forty tackles.

Playing in the NFL opened my eyes to a lot of things. These guys worked hard at their craft. Everybody had the drive to be the best. In addition to the physicality of the league, I was amazed at the spirituality. Previously in my life, I believed Christians were weak-minded, feeble individuals who needed help. But when I walked into the Jacksonville Jaguars locker room, I found strong, healthy, wealthy, and dedicated followers of Christ. They weren't weak at all. Even our chaplain at Jacksonville was a stud! Anthony "AJ" Johnson had

played running back in the NFL for eleven years. As the Jaguars chaplain, he helped me overcome my hatred. AJ asked me one simple question that I'll never forget: "If you had not gone through the things that you went through, could you possibly stand here today and be the person that you are?" From that moment on, instead of hating where I'd come from and being envious of other kids, I learned to be gracious and appreciative of what I'd gone through. AJ was right: My experiences had molded me into the man I'd become.

Don (26) as a Lion, tackling Ted Ginn during a game against the Saints
>> Stephen Lew/CSM/Shutterstock

AJ also planted a seed, like Jesus described in the parable of the sower in Mark 4. Though Chaplain Johnson never got to see his example and words take root in my life, because in 2011, I became a Detroit Lion.

It took two years until I surrendered my life to Christ. During that time, I read and learned about many of the world's religions. Some offered a degree of helpful advice and solace. But, ultimately, only Christianity provided the love, peace, forgiveness, and joy that was missing in my life. The Bible answered all my questions and motivated me to take a leap of faith.

Once I accepted Jesus into my life, it didn't improve my game on the field. So I don't want anybody to think that if they become a Christian, God is going to do something good for them. That's not a strong starting base for following God. The only place to start a relationship with God is by humbling yourself and knowing we are all sinners and Jesus Christ died on the cross for our sins. To be a Christian means that you believe in the death, burial, and resurrection of Jesus Christ. Faith in him alone provides our salvation. When I meet people, I want to make the gospel relatable to what they are dealing with. I'm living proof that no matter what you are going through, there is a better way in Christ. For that reason, I'm open and unashamed of my belief in Jesus Christ.

Don (center) listens with classmates during a class at the Moody Theological Seminary

>> Carlos Osorio/AP/Shutterstock

While accepting Christ didn't make me a better football player, it *did* make me a better person. I treated people the way they deserved and became a team leader. I played with the Lions for seven seasons and became one of the most respected special teams players in the game. As a gunner on punts, I often faced two or three blockers as I sprinted down the field in kick coverage. I had to be adaptable and persevere to make it to my goal.

And the same thing is true in my faith. Following Christ takes perseverance. I'm constantly learning new things. For example, while playing in Detroit, I also started studying to receive a master's degree in Theological Studies with a focus on the Old Testament from Moody Theological Seminary.

During the 2018 offseason, I became a free agent and was picked up by Jacksonville. That's where my professional football and faith journey began. Unfortunately, I injured myself in the preseason, and am now a free agent once again. I don't know exactly what my next step is in life, but I do know this: No matter what you are going through, God has a plan for you.

A **NEW** CREATION

Trying to come up with *one* favorite Bible verse isn't easy. I've committed a lot of Scripture to memory. First Corinthians 15 is an amazing chapter, talking about the death and resurrection of Christ. That's the core of Christianity. Our hope is in Christ. But one of my favorite passage from God's Word is 2 Corinthians 5:17–21 (NKJV), which starts, "If anyone is in Christ, he is a new creation; old things have passed away; behold, all things have become new." We are not here by accident. God makes us new and wants us to tell others about him. He fights for us! He makes us righteous. He gives purpose to life that can only be fulfilled through Christ.

CHAPTER 11

AP/Shutterstock

MILES KILLEBREW
It's All About Relationships

@MilesKillebrew my brother in Christ 4 life!! From competing against each other . . . to our trip to Israel! Ha, ha it was LIT! Getting baptized in the Jordan River. Workouts on the beach. Memories for a lifetime! #CanYouGoWhenYoureTired #DoYouNeedSomeTapeForYourHeart hahaha S/O to Earl!!! #WOC

Southern Utah University	Henderson, NV	Safety

When Miles Killebrew came into the league in 2016, NFL Network draft analyst Mike Mayock called him "the best hitter in the draft." At 6'2" tall and 220 pounds, Miles shined at the NFL Combine. Not only did he impress with his physicality, he also stood out with his intelligence. His Wonderlic Test score of 38 was the highest of any safety in the draft. That score also placed him in the 98th percentile of anybody who's ever taken the intelligence test. Chemists have an average Wonderlic score of 31. Miles blew that up, just like he's known for blowing up running backs, receivers, and tight ends with his big hits at safety.

I couldn't believe what I was hearing.

A coach for the Lions looked me right in the eye and said, "We don't think you're a fit in Detroit, and we aren't interested in drafting you."

Sitting across from the Detroit coaches at the 2016 Senior Bowl, I tried not to show my shock. This was supposed to be a job interview. But it wasn't going like any interview I'd ever had before.

Why would they request a meeting just to say they weren't interested? I wondered.

I didn't know how to react. Pulling it together, I calmly replied, "Okay, was there anything else you wanted to ask me?" There wasn't. We exchanged goodbyes, and I left.

Walking away from the meeting, I was disappointed. Having someone say to your face, "We don't want you at all," is tough. If they didn't want me, what about the other thirty-one NFL teams?

But it turned out it was all just a test. Three months later, the Lions selected me in the fourth round of the NFL Draft. That's when I learned my reaction had impressed the coaches.

Miles (35, top) helping take down the Packers' Ty Montgomery during a game for the NFC North title
>> Duane Burleson/AP/Shutterstock

I got the call as I was driving to my graduation ceremony at Southern Utah University (SUU). Not only did I walk across the stage to receive my degree in engineering that day, I also got my dream job in the NFL.

FINDING FOCUS

Growing up in Las Vegas, temptation is all around. Sin City lives up to its name. This is where people come to party. But I was never really tempted by the party lifestyle.

My parents explained to me at a young age that the people I hung out with would rub off on me. It was like I would exchange a piece of me with a piece of them. That bit of wisdom made me very conscious to hang around people who had goals similar to mine. And because I grew up in the church, that's where I lot of my friends came from.

After graduating high school, I wasn't as wise about choosing my friends. I attended SUU and played football for the Thunderbirds. Once I arrived in Cedar City, Utah, there was so much more freedom! No curfew. No one to answer to. I was excited to be out on my own.

With all this new freedom and with no one to hold me accountable, I started giving in to the temptations of college life. I went to a lot of parties and went out with a ton of girls. I stopped going to church, because most of the people I hung around with didn't seem to care about God. All the late nights made getting up in the morning difficult. I began not showing up for class. My grades had always been important to me, but since I wasn't attending the lectures, my classwork struggled.

Instead of bringing me happiness, partying and dating around left me feeling dark and empty inside. At one point I was in a relationship with a non-Christian girl. She was both beautiful and popular, but her goals and values didn't line up with mine. It was weird because I couldn't be myself around her. All I felt was stress! We couldn't talk about anything real. It was all superficial.

It was like I was square peg trying to fit into a round hole. I thought freedom meant I could do whatever I wanted . . . but that was a trap. True freedom is only found in Christ. I knew I couldn't get out of this difficult time on my own, so I decided to go back to what I knew was real—and that was God.

My parents quoted this verse to me all the time growing up, but it's so true: "Start children off on the way they should go, and even when they are old they will not turn from it" (Proverbs 22:6). God was calling me back. I started looking around campus for guys who were on the path I wanted to be on. And I didn't have to look far.

> **I THOUGHT FREEDOM MEANT I COULD DO WHATEVER I WANTED . . . BUT THAT WAS A TRAP.**

Rodain Delus was one of my college roommates. At first, we weren't even close. I'd just see him in passing. But then I noticed Rodain was going to church. He was joyful, while I felt imprisoned in sin.

Breaking out of my bad patterns wasn't easy. For a while, it was a constant battle. On one side, I saw Rodain. He was doing the things I wanted to be doing. On the other side were the influences that pulled me away from the positive path. In my second year of college, I was at a complete and total loss. That's when I decided to rededicate my life to Christ.

Rodain and I started a Bible study with a few other guys from campus. What I discovered in the process was a common theme among people at SUU. I felt like everybody came to college with a mindset of being free and spending the next four years doing whatever they wanted. Instead of "making the most" of their time, they ended up wasting their time.

Not everyone who came to the Bible study was a Christian. But as time progressed, every member of the group came to Christ. We were tight.

It was only about four to six guys, but being around them gave me so much encouragement. The small group size allowed all of us to be more vulnerable with each other. We knew it was a safe place to discuss anything we were going through. Before we even realized it, that type of transparency was changing our lives.

We were a band of brothers. I had grown up with a similar support system: My parents supported my dreams and my walk with Christ. My friends were a positive influence as well; so was my sister. When I lost that at college, I was lost. But our Bible study helped me feel grounded again, like I could be myself. They all wanted me to be successful, and I was back on the right path. It showed on the football field too.

THE **RIGHT** PATH

Once I was centered on the path that God intended for me, I was reminded of the wisdom that's contained in my favorite Bible verse, Proverbs 3:5–7. It states, "Trust in the Lord with all your heart and lean not on your own understanding; in all your ways submit to him, and he will make your paths straight. Do not be wise in your own eyes; fear the Lord and shun evil."

God wants 100 percent of our heart. All of it! We can't give God anything less. Sometimes I tend to rely on my own understanding. My pride will take me down a path that's filled with twists. My dad was the same way. But that's no excuse. I have to constantly remind myself to submit to God and his will. When I do that, God keeps me on the straight path and away from evil.

During my junior year at Southern Utah, I recorded 101 tackles. I also made four fumble recoveries and intercepted three passes—one of which I took to the house. A pick-six can change a game, and so can a bone-jarring hit. My senior season was filled with big tackles—I made 132 of them. I also broke up a pass in more than half of my games and blocked two kicks on special teams.

My on-field exploits definitely caught the eye of NFL scouts.

INTO THE LIONS' DEN

After my performances at the Senior Bowl and the NFL Combine, some draft experts had me going as high as the second or third round. I tried not to get caught up in the hype. Besides, I was pretty busy. After slacking at the beginning of my college career, I had to hit the books hard to graduate with an engineering degree, while still putting in the time on the football field and in the training facility.

Still, I'm human. I have moments when I feel insecure and down on my myself. We all get nervous or fearful of what may come next in life. But in those hard times that would ordinarily cause fear, that's when God ultimately receives his glory. I've seen people go through times of hardship, and God has used those moments to bring them to him. God's grace in the world is amazing.

So when I go through times of uncertainty, like during the NFL Draft, it's not a lack of fear that keeps me calm—it's a realization of love. From this point of understanding, I'm able to see football and my NFL career in a more businesslike way. Because faith in God's love is my foundation, I don't need to find my worth in coaches liking me or wanting me to be on their team. I can't get frustrated when my body breaks down or I get hurt. My job in the NFL doesn't give me security. The only thing I can count on is God.

Being focused on God also keeps me humble. Pride can be a big problem among professional athletes. It's easy for us players to start thinking more of ourselves than we should. We can start looking down on other people. But Jesus didn't look down on people. He loved them and built them up.

Miles goes up against Kori Garcia in a game against Cal Poly

›› Laura Dickinson/*The Tribune*/AP Images

I want to share the life, the love, and the grace God constantly offers to everyone. In fact, taking God to a hurting world and telling people about Christ is a driving force for me. Being a Christian is the most important part of my life!

I didn't always feel that way. And I had to learn some lessons the hard way. Like the Bible says, "A man reaps what he sows" (Galatians 6:7). That verse and the ones that come next give great insight into God's view of how we behave. Our actions matter. If we do things that please the flesh, we reap destruction. But if our actions please the Holy Spirit, we reap eternal life. In addition, the seeds of love we sow in those around us ultimately return more fruit than we originally planted. Basically, if we love those around us as Christ loves us, we will see that mirrored back to us exponentially.

I first learned this mindset from my parents. Their constant guidance has ushered me toward a relationship-minded view of the world instead of a me-first view. But I realize not everybody comes from the type of household I came from. Many people come from dysfunctional families or no family at all, growing up through the foster care system. They may feel empty or disconnected from the world. My advice to everyone is to find a support system with friends that value your success. We all need people we can rely on and who point us in the right direction. If not friends, then maybe a mentor or a teacher you can trust. Most importantly, the only thing that can fill in the missing hole in our lives is God. God is the ultimate Father. And God's family is huge. He wants everyone to become one of his children.

I still remember what it first felt like when I prayed to have a personal relationship with Jesus. This may sound weird, but it's like when you meet a cute girl for the first time and you cannot get her off your mind. All you can do is think about her. You get all excited and

> **WE ALL NEED PEOPLE WE CAN RELY ON AND WHO POINT US IN THE RIGHT DIRECTION.**

hyped and feel so warm inside at the thought or mention of her. I'm laughing when I say that, but, honestly, that's what it feels like to be a Christian.

Having a relationship with Christ *is* the most important thing. But also value the relationships around you. The strength and comfort you get from close family and friends is something you cannot calculate. Show love to the people in your life. It doesn't have to be a grand gesture. It can be as simple as genuinely listening to someone over a cup of coffee. Taking care of each other is just something that Christians do. It's what my parents did. It's what my friends in Bible study did. And it's what my brothers in the NFL do as well. Their positive impact on me makes me want to positively impact people in return. Because life is all about relationships.

CHAPTER 12

BRANDON MARSHALL
Redemption

@**BMarshall** Man, when I first met you I was a little starstruck, honestly. The fan in me wanted your autograph . . . haha. But I definitely look up to you bro. You motivate me to keep going in life! Not only as a football player, but as a brother in Christ and a great family man! #NeedThatJerseySwap haha!

| University of Central Florida | Pittsburgh, PA | Wide Receiver |

There is so much more to Brandon Marshall than just his otherworldly football skills. He is thoughtful and articulate. He's not afraid to share his thoughts and opinions with the media. He's willing to stand up and tell the world that he's a believer in Jesus Christ. Brandon has a big heart and big platform that he's built through more than twelve amazing seasons in the NFL.

There is little doubt amongst football analysts that Brandon will go down as one of the greatest wide receivers in the history of professional football. Entering the 2018 season, he's already in the top 20 all-time in career receptions, and he's just outside the top 20 in receiving yards with 12,215. He has posted eight seasons of more than 1,000 receiving yards, including seven in a row. Brandon has been selected to the Pro Bowl six times and has twice been named All-Pro—first-team in 2012 and second-team in 2015. He also holds two NFL receiving records that will be hard to beat. On December 13, 2009, Brandon pulled in twenty-one receptions in a single game when he was a member of the Denver Broncos. That's a pretty good *month* for many wideouts! He also has surpassed one thousand receiving yards in a season for four different teams.

One of Brandon's record twenty-one catches during his game on December 13, 2009

» Joe Amon/*The Denver Post* via Getty Images

Brandon entered the league in 2006 as a rather unheralded fourth-round draft pick from the University of Central Florida. At 6'5" and 230 pounds, the Broncos liked his size and playmaking ability. Through the years, he's made routine catches look easy and seemingly impossible catches look routine. After beginning his NFL career in Denver, Brandon's played for the Miami Dolphins, Chicago Bears, New York Jets, and New York Giants. During the 2018 offseason, Brandon signed with the Seattle Seahawks. Opposing defensive backs and linebackers talk about his ability to break tackles after catching the ball and his physicality to win battles in the air. As impressive as his strength on the field is, the strength of his faith in God is even more impactful.

At the age of twenty-six, I was introduced to the word *repentance*. I never really understood what the word meant until a buddy of mine sat me down in my living room in Orlando, Florida. He explained that repentance was "changing your mind." It was turning away from sin and turning toward God. At that moment, I knew what Christianity was all about. Still, another year passed before I truly gave my life to Christ.

I was twenty-seven when I finally realized that Christianity wasn't just a belief, it was a lifestyle. My journey to accept Jesus Christ as my Savior, however, began years before. I grew up in a community in Pittsburgh, Pennsylvania, that was very volatile. A lot of distress, fighting, and drug dealing. But growing up, I was always intrigued by a few men in my life. Not by their strength or the fear they commanded in the neighborhood, but in the way these men worshiped Jesus. Back in elementary school, I would see my pastor

Brandon (right) with his dad during his senior year of high school.

>> Photo courtesy of Brandon Marshall

and my father worship in church. That made a huge impact in my life. At Lake Howell High School in Florida, our backup quarterback was on fire for Christ. In college, our tight end loved the Lord. In the NFL, strong Christians like Brian Dawkins of the Denver Broncos stood out in a crowded locker room. It made me curious.

But for so long I was blind and didn't understand what Christianity really was. I simply thought, *I go to church, so I'm a Christian.* Some people say they believe in Jesus and go to church, but their lifestyle doesn't reflect the values God wants us to reflect. I came to the conclusion that I have to be either all in or all out. Knowing the importance of repentance, and realizing that Christianity isn't a word but a lifestyle, meant that I had to turn and walk away from the things that were not of God. We all know what those things are. By hearing me say that, you may even begin to feel convicted—especially if you have been

Brandon (6) catching a pass during the Citrus Bowl
>> Central Florida/Collegiate Images/Getty Images

doing something you know is not right. But there was no way I could say I was a Christian if my walk and my talk didn't reflect that.

One of the reasons professional athletes are so mentally unhealthy after the game is taken away from them and they retire is that they suddenly have no identity. All our lives, we are put on a pedestal. We are told what our purpose is.

PASSING **THE** TEST

My favorite Bible verse is James 1:2–4: "Consider it pure joy, my brothers and sisters, whenever you face trials of many kinds, because you know that the testing of your faith produces perseverance. Let perseverance finish its work so that you may be mature and complete, not lacking anything." I've faced many trials. When I was aimlessly wandering in life, I wrapped my arms around this verse. This passage gave me the understanding that if I would just seek God and worship him, I would come through my trials as a better person and a better Christian.

Basically, I was told that I existed to catch a football. Once I realized that football wasn't my purpose, but instead was merely a platform God gave me to advance his kingdom and to spread the gospel, I was able to relax. Then I knew it wasn't about me anymore. Catching a football really means nothing in the grand scheme of things.

It's not that I don't love football. Where I grew up, football was a way of life. It was the culture. People didn't care about basketball. And forget about soccer and baseball. I can't even remember not having a football cradled in my arms or not being part of the game. It's part of my DNA. That's why I'm super passionate about it. So passionate, in fact, that sometimes I cross the line. When I feel myself getting close to that line, or even when I cross that line, my faith always brings me back. Now it's not about the contract, it's not about the fame, it's not about the money, and it's not about the wins or losses. It is about using this platform to lead someone else to Christ.

So whether you're a youth, teenager, or older, I want to tell you to show up! Many people, myself included, are afraid to take that step of faith. We think we have to give up everything—we can't talk to girls, we can't have fun, we can't do this or that. But the reality is that the opposite happens. When you give yourself up to God, you get so much more. Show up, take baby steps, and find a good church. Seek out a great mentor who studies the Word of God and can teach you what Christianity is all about. And pray for clarity when it comes to God's plan for your life. For me, understanding redemption led to repentance and a new life in Christ. The old is gone. I'm a different person than I was five or six years ago. Past mistakes are forgiven. And you can find that new life too.

**Brandon (with ball) being tackled by Champ Bailey—
one of his role models—after becoming a Dolphin**

>> Wilfredo Lee/AP/Shutterstock

CHAPTER 13

LORENZO ALEXANDER
One Man Gang

@onemangang97 All I know is whenever I see you on the field, you're playing with a purpose. By the way you play I know you have been through some ups and downs. You are so respected by so many people in this league. But I respect you because of the people you've proved wrong along the way. #onemangang #WPMOY You motivated me to be GREAT bro! #FaithMotivated

University of California, Berkeley	Oakland, CA	Linebacker

Lorenzo Alexander set the NFL on fire during the 2016 season. The Buffalo Bills linebacker finished third in the league in sacks with 12.5. He also forced three fumbles, which doubled his career total. And if that wasn't enough, he got his first career interception.

Some called it a fairy-tale season. But Lorenzo's NFL career has been anything but a fairy tale. You've heard the saying, "Third time's a charm." For Lorenzo, it was more like "Sixth time's a charm." Prior to 2016, Lorenzo had played for Carolina, Baltimore, Washington, Arizona, and Oakland. Through nine previous seasons, he'd notched just nine sacks and forced three fumbles. His epic 2016 performance led to his second selection to the Pro Bowl and his first nomination as a second-team All-Pro. Many wondered how he had such a great year. The answer might sound obvious, but Lorenzo simply took advantage of an opportunity God gave him.

I never tried to earn the nickname "One Man Gang." But during my third year in the NFL, the Washington Redskins played me on special teams, offensive line, fullback, defensive end, and defensive tackle. Now as I enter the 2018 season, I've added inside linebacker and outside linebacker. In my thirteen years in the league, I've shown the versatility to play whatever role was going to help my team. I guess that's why my Redskins teammates started calling me a "One Man Gang."

Lorenzo (97) ready to take the field, alongside teammates Kedric Golston and Chris Wilson
>> Pablo Martinez Monsivais/AP/Shutterstock

My plan coming into the NFL was to be a dominating defensive tackle. That's what I was at the University of California. There, I was a two-time honorable mention defensive lineman in the Pac-10. At 6'1", 315 pounds, most teams double-teamed me with two blockers. I figured I'd get drafted, go to the NFL, and become one of the league's best.

God had other plans. Although I didn't know Jesus as my personal Savior yet, he gave me a reality check. It started on draft day, 2005.

Growing up in Oakland, California, I was raised by a single mother. Despite that fact, I didn't lack for a male role model. My maternal uncle, Steven Moore, treated me as if I was his own child. My uncle was my coach, substitute father, and the protector of my mind and heart. So on draft day, I was at my uncle's house, surrounded by family. I was confident I'd be drafted.

After the first few rounds of the draft, I got a call from a team saying I'd be their next pick. I watched the TV, ready for my dream to come true. The team's pick got posted . . . and it wasn't me. I sat there in disbelief. I was angry. I couldn't believe I'd been lied to. Once the draft was over, my agent called. Buffalo, Carolina, and San Diego were all interested in signing me as an undrafted free agent. I didn't want to waste any time. The Panthers had the best defensive scheme for my talents, so I chose Carolina.

The Panthers cut me twice: once in 2005 and again in 2006, after I'd spent a year on their practice squad. The Baltimore Ravens picked me up for their practice squad, but in the sometimes-crazy world of the NFL, I was released five days later. I ended up spending the season on the Washington Redskins practice squad. In 2007, I made my NFL debut. The Redskins had asked me to move to offensive line, and I also excelled on special teams. After three seasons playing those positions, Washington changed its coaching staff and defensive scheme. The new coaches thought I could play linebacker in a 3–4 defense—an alignment made up of three linemen and four linebackers. But the offer came with a condition: I had to slim down to 240 pounds.

I don't know if I would have been able to lose the weight if I hadn't found something a couple seasons earlier: God. I went to church with my grandmother while I was growing up, but it was simply something I did. It had no real meaning to me. That wasn't the case for some of my Washington teammates. God meant *everything* to them. Antwaan Randle El, James Thrash, Renaldo Wynn, and Kedric Golston were four guys who played and lived with integrity. They showed me the Bible was real through their actions. They lived the life of a believer and a follower of Christ. They walked the talk. I got to know these guys the same year our teammate Sean Taylor was murdered after five men broke into his house looking to steal cash. After that event, I began to wonder what my life was all about. *What am I living for? Who am I impacting? What is my legacy?* By the end of the 2007 season, I decided to give my life to Christ.

WHAT AM I LIVING FOR? WHO AM I IMPACTING? WHAT IS MY LEGACY?

From the time I prayed to receive Jesus Christ as my Savior, God began making changes in my spiritual life. Then I had to make changes in my physical life. Right away, I ramped up my training. I started biking and doing MMA workouts. I cut out fast food and went on a strict diet. Eventually, I got down to 240 pounds and earned a spot at linebacker.

Despite playing well, the Redskins already had three Pro Bowl linebackers—London Fletcher, Ryan Kerrigan, and Brian Orakpo. In 2011, I was back on special teams. I was disappointed, but I took pride in doing my job and playing my role on the team. I made the Pro Bowl for my special teams play in 2012. Things were going well in Washington. I enjoyed my teammates, coaches, and fans. But Washington chose not to re-sign me after the 2012 season. I knew it was a business decision, but it still hurt.

In 2013, the Arizona Cardinals offered me a contract. I was excited to head back west and compete for a starting job at linebacker. But in my third game with the Cardinals, I tore a tendon in my left foot. My season was over, and Arizona put me on injured reserve. I immediately focused my energies on working hard to rehab the injury so I could be back on the field in 2014. I did make it back, but my foot didn't feel right. I didn't have the same explosion I had once possessed. Not surprisingly, Arizona let me go. That's when I ended up with the Oakland Raiders, my hometown team.

BACK IN OAKLAND FOR GOOD

When I was growing up, the Raiders played in Los Angeles, so I was more of a San Francisco 49ers fan. But coming back to Oakland had its perks. In 2008, I had started the Lorenzo Alexander ACES Foundation. Its purpose was to run programs that enriched the lives of Oakland-area youths and helped them understand they could achieve their goals and dreams. Now I was playing for the Black and Silver.

Lorenzo with some of the kids who took part in the ACES Foundation

>> Courtesy of Lorenzo Alexander and the ACES Foundation

NO **FEAR**

One of my favorite verses is 2 Timothy 1:7, which says, "For the Spirit God gave us does not make us timid, but gives us power, love and self-discipline." This verse daily reminds me to rely on God and to not be afraid. Don't be passive and timid. That is not from God. Power, love, and a sound mind are not soft and lazy. Rather, these attributes allow you to be your best. You have God, a solid-rock foundation in your life; you don't need to fear anything.

It was great being able to help those kids. And I soon discovered that God had an even bigger reason for me to return to Oakland. During that time, my cousin was released from prison after being incarcerated for ten years. He and I were close as kids. We were like brothers. It was important for me to help him get his life together when he was released, and God put me there!

God was also doing big things for me on the field. As the season progressed in Oakland, my foot started to feel better. My explosiveness came back. I felt like my old self again.

When the season ended, I started looking for teams that would give me another shot at linebacker. Only Buffalo seemed interested in working me in on defense. I signed with the Bills and made the most of it.

Throughout my career, I've played whatever position my coaches asked me to play. That versatility led me to being a Pro Bowler and an All-Pro.

I want to show that same versatility as a follower of Christ. I want to do whatever I can to lead others into a personal relationship with Jesus.

Lorenzo (left) tackling Dede Westbrook during a January 2018 NFL wildcard game against the Jaguars

>> Phelan M. Ebenhack/AP/Shutterstock

In the book of James, it says faith without deeds is useless. In other words, as Christians, our actions and words should be a reflection of Christ. I can tell by my actions, by my works, if I am reading my Bible often enough. When I am close with God in my daily walk, I act differently toward my wife and children, as well as toward other people. My works tell me if my faith is lined up properly.

When I was a kid, some of my coaches would tell me to get mad and play angry. Once I accepted the Lord as my Savior, I played to honor him. I don't play mad anymore. This makes me a more consistent individual and a better player. Based on my God-given talent, compared to others in the NFL I'm somewhere near the bottom. But by tapping into God's Spirit on the field, I am able to accomplish through him things that are well beyond my abilities. I give all glory to him for that.

My desire is for others to see Christ through my actions, just as I saw God through the actions of some of my Washington teammates. I hope you make that your desire as well. God made you in his own image. Surround yourself with the right people, love others, and have a positive spirit. Some people may never read the Bible. The only Bible they'll ever see is you. Serve others, build relationships, and don't judge. Feed yourself with the Word of God—what you nourish your spirit with is what comes out of you. And if you do that, you too might become a One Man Gang for Jesus.

Lorenzo and his family

≫ Photo courtesy of Lorenzo Alexander

CHAPTER 14

Adam Hunger/AP/
Shutterstock

CHARLES JOHNSON

It's Okay to Be Different

@MrInkredibleXII Man, we have known each other forever now. I literally want to see us both make it BIG in this league. We both undrafted and trust in the Lord for everything. We just gotta keep going bro! Keep that chip on your shoulder.

Grand Valley State University	Elsmere, KY	Wide Receiver

Charles Johnson didn't start playing football until his junior year of high school. He grew up starring on the baseball field. As a shortstop and pitcher, he was one of the best players at Lloyd Memorial High in Erlanger, Kentucky. At 6'2" and 185 pounds, his athletic talents helped him shine in basketball and track too. But once he stepped onto a football field, he knew he'd found his calling.

As a junior, Charles caught twenty-six passes for the Juggernauts, amassing six hundred yards and six touchdowns. His senior season was just as good. In 2007, he signed a football scholarship to play at Eastern Kentucky University, but was suspended from school after a couple of years. Through a series of what could only be God-ordained events, he landed at Grand Valley State University in Allendale, Michigan, and caught fifty-six passes for fifteen touchdowns and more than one thousand yards. Following two solid years at Grand Valley, the Green Bay Packers drafted Charles in the seventh round of the 2013 draft. As he entered the 2018 season, Charles battled for a spot with the New York Jets after seeing time with the Packers, Cleveland Brown, Minnesota Vikings, and Carolina Panthers. In a word, Charles' path to the NFL has been *different*. And in his case, different is good.

Charles during his Juggernaut days

>> Photo courtesy of Charles Johnson

I had just been suspended by Eastern Kentucky University. My football scholarship was gone. My goal of playing in the NFL looked like it might not ever happen. I'd played well on the field for the Colonels. But I'd gotten in trouble off the field for some dumb decisions. Silly things, like taking the couch out of the dorm lobby and putting it in our room. Another time, my friends and I got written up for having a fight with fire extinguishers in the hallway. I was upset when I started driving home, no longer a student at Eastern Kentucky, so it seemed fitting when it started to rain.

I was going about eighty miles per hour in the fast lane of the interstate when the rain began. I tapped on the brakes to get out of cruise control. Suddenly, my car started to hydroplane. The tail of the car spun around, hitting the concrete retaining wall that divided the highway. Now I was going backward on the highway and facing oncoming traffic. I looked through the rain-splattered windshield and saw two semi-trailer trucks coming straight toward me. I uttered a fast prayer to God to spare my life as the two trucks parted like the Red Sea. *Zoom, zoom!* They roared by me on either side. Finally, I came to a stop and was able to safely drive to the side of the road. I was crying. I knew I could've died, but God was with me. He kept me from death.

I had already gone through many struggles in life. My parents divorced when I was young. I chose to live with my father; my brother stayed with my mom. My dad was a hardworking man, but his life was difficult, especially when he had to move to Cincinnati due to an illness. I went to live with my mother for a year. During this time, my brother's girlfriend began taking me to church with her. I met a family at church and became close with other godly friends. From there, I started attending Young Life meetings in the evening and church on the weekend. Pretty soon, I made a decision to follow Christ and was baptized.

Charles (right) with his dad
>> Photo courtesy of Charles Johnson

While my eternity was secure, my life was still in turmoil. There was so much uncertainty in my family and for my future that I temporarily lost sight of Christ. At one point, I left home and spent nights sleeping on a friend's couch. I didn't want to be a drain on his family, so I found my food in dumpsters during the day. I was running from God, but God stayed right next to me. The parents of the friend I was staying with were strong believers. In fact, my friend's father was a pastor and his mother was deeply involved in church programs. They invited me to stay with them. I went to church with them twice a week. Every message that the pastor gave from the pulpit spoke directly to my heart.

AWAY FROM MY KENTUCKY HOME

After my suspension from Eastern Kentucky University, I transferred to Antelope Valley College in Lancaster, California. I was farther away from home than I'd ever been, but junior college was my only option. This could've been the worst time of my life, but God had other plans. While I was in California, I met Kalyn. She's now my wife and the mother of my three beautiful daughters and son. I also had a great year on the football field. Things looked up, but then life took another twist.

My father got ill again. I chose to return to Kentucky to care for him. I had to take two jobs to pay his bills—one making sandwiches at Arby's and a second job as a host at Olive Garden. I was also taking classes at a local community college to finish my degree and working out, because I knew I wanted to get back to football.

The following year I earned a spot at Grand Valley State University, a Division II school in Allendale, Michigan. In two seasons at GVSU, I pulled in 128 passes and thirty-one touchdowns. My statistics were good, but NFL teams don't often seriously look at Division II players. I wasn't invited to the NFL Combine, but my 40-yard dash and vertical leap at my school's Pro Day were off the charts. In the 2013 NFL Draft, the Green Bay Packers selected me in the seventh round.

Charles (with ball) in a game against Michigan
Tech, where he had seven catches for 165 yards,
and scored three first-half touchdowns

➤➤ MLive/Advance Media

Getting drafted was a high point. But I've experienced many ups and downs since that day. A knee injury hampered my performance in Packers training camp. They ended up putting me on the practice squad. Then six weeks into the 2013 season, Cleveland claimed me. The Browns training staff and doctors discovered my knee injury was worse than they thought. I had a torn ACL and would require season-ending surgery.

In September 2014, the Minnesota Vikings plucked me off the Browns' practice roster. After being inactive the first two games of the season, I began to flourish. I played in eleven games, starting six of them, where I caught thirty-one passes for 475 yards. I played three years in Minnesota, going from one of the top receiving targets to injured and back again. After battling so many injuries—including another knee injury that kept me off the field after signing with the Carolina Panthers in 2017—I have to remind myself to continue to work hard and believe in God's plan.

Coaches used to tell me, "Remember that someone else is repping your max." In other words, there are stronger players out there. It's a reminder that talent doesn't always win; hard work beats talent when talent doesn't work hard! And nothing can get in the way of God's plan for me. Someone much bigger than myself is looking out for me. I have a strong faith, and I know that he is there for me through the positive times and especially in the negatives times—and I've had plenty of both.

Doing well on the football field is important to me. But I love being a husband and a dad even more than I love playing football, which is a lot.

COMFORT **AND** STRENGTH

I have two Bible verses that are particularly important to me. The first is Jeremiah 29:11: "'For I know the plans I have for you,' declares the Lord, 'plans to prosper you and not to harm you, plans to give you hope and a future.'" I take comfort in the fact that God is here to protect me and care for my future. The second verse is Philippians 4:13: "I can do all this through him who gives me strength." As an NFL player, you're in trouble if you don't believe in your athletic gifts. This promise in the Bible gives me confidence in my abilities, knowing that the Lord God Almighty tells me I can accomplish anything.

I know I'll never be perfect in either role—only Christ is perfect—but I'm teaching my kids about God and have them in church regularly. My purpose goes beyond the field. I live to follow Christ and love others. Without faith, there is no life.

My advice is to do the things no one else is doing. Be different from the world! It's okay to be smart. It's okay to go to church. It's okay to love God. I've always done things differently, and I know God loves that.

Charles Johnson (12) pulls in a touchdown against the Green Bay Packers

>> Adam Bettcher/Getty Images

CHAPTER 15

JORDAN MATTHEWS

Identity Crisis

@jmattjmattjmatt I know it's old but you and Carson Wentz had the dopest TD celebration in the league 2 years ago haha!! From Vandy to the league, man I respect you more than you would ever know because you a real dude, and not many of us are out here! Continue to be great bro! But if we ever meet in the middle of the field, don't be mad at me after the game haha!

Vanderbilt	Madison, AL	Wide Receiver

Jordan Matthews' first three seasons in the NFL couldn't have gone much better. The second-round draft pick flew high for the Philadelphia Eagles from 2014 to 2016. He had 225 catches for nearly 2,700 yards, and nineteen touchdowns! In fact, the July 2016 issue of *Sports Illustrated* rated Jordan as the fourth-best slot receiver in the entire NFL.

After being traded to the Buffalo Bills, Jordan struggled through a forgettable season of injuries and drops. Heading into the 2018 season, the free agent had a decision to make. Arizona, Green Bay, Tennessee, and New England were interested in signing the dynamic receiver. Which team would he choose? His decision to sign with the Patriots can be summed up in two words: Tom Brady. Who wouldn't want to play with possibly the best quarterback ever to spin a pigskin? Brady has made many slot receivers great, including Danny Amendola, who moved to the Miami Dolphins in the off-season.

Unfortunately, Jordan suffered an injury in the preseason and was cut from the Patriots before the 2018 season could really start. But Jordan isn't one to give up, and he also knows life is about more than football. And now he has an opportunity with an old team, the Philadelphia Eagles—who defeated the Patriots in Super Bowl LII.

At 6'3" and 212 pounds, Jordan has good size for a slot receiver. Jordan's early years with the Eagles were huge, but his biggest years could be right around the corner.

Jordan, practicing with the Patriots during the 2018 preseason

›› AP/Charles Krupa/Shutterstock

Humility. It's not a trait used to describe most athletes. When you're told from an early age that you're great, it's easy to start believing it. There have been times when it's been tempting to think, *I'm all that.* But I've had great examples in my life of what it means to be truly humble.

First, there's my family. I was blessed to be raised in a two-parent household. My parents were successful and supportive, and they always made time for me. They rarely missed any of my sporting events from high school through college. They even attend my NFL games. I know many kids lack that support. My situation was idyllic. I owe much of my success to my family, and that keeps me humble.

Next, there's my mother's first cousin, Jerry Rice. Yes, *that* Jerry Rice, the Hall of Fame wide receiver. The GOAT. Nobody in the history of the NFL has more receptions, receiving yards, or touchdown receptions. If anybody has reason to boast, it's him. Yet throughout his career and even today, he's remained humble. He's a great example to me.

Last, and most important, is my Savior Jesus Christ. Both of my parents believe in Jesus. I attended a Christian school and was immersed in the Word of God from a young age. I went to chapel at school Monday through Friday. Then on Sundays, I went to church. So I learned a lot about the Bible and Jesus whether I wanted to or not! The Word of God is a two-edged sword, and it's going to pierce you after a while. Jesus was God, but

Jordan in his early playing days, wearing his great-cousin Jerry Rice's jersey number
>> Photo courtesy of Jordan Matthews

he came to earth to serve, not to be served. He died on the cross for my sins and the sins of the world. Talk about humility!

Being a Christian doesn't mean that everything is perfect. It doesn't even mean that you'll be perfect. But it does mean that you follow a perfect God who has a plan for your life.

Sometimes it's been hard for me to see that plan. Coming out of high school, I didn't have any college scholarship offers. I'd been an all-state wide receiver at Madison Academy in Alabama during my senior year. Then Vanderbilt made me a late offer. Not only did Vanderbilt play against the best competition in the SEC, it also had great academics. I knew it'd be the perfect place for me. The waiting for my chance to shine was hard, but it taught me a lot about patience and waiting for God's timing.

THE WAITING FOR MY CHANCE TO SHINE WAS HARD.

It also me taught me the rewards of hard work. I wanted to be the hardest worker on the team. As a true freshman, I saw limited action, but still managed to make fifteen catches, including four touchdowns. From there, my numbers just exploded. I had 778 receiving yards as a sophomore, and then averaged more than one hundred catches and 1,400 yards during my junior and senior years. By the time I graduated, I went from a virtually unwanted high school player to the career record-holder for catches and receiving yards in the SEC. Only through God's grace could something like that happen. I mean, sometimes it's still hard for me to wrap my mind around. But God is the only reason I had the success I did at Vandy. I'm so thankful to him for it.

After Philadelphia drafted me in the second round, I went on to have a great rookie year with the Eagles. In my second season, I struggled a little, if you can call nearly one thousand receiving yards a struggle. But the media soured on me. Fans even turned on me. Philadelphia fans are among the most passionate in the NFL. If they're not happy with you, you'll hear about it. Eventually, I got down on myself. I let the negativity affect my performance. During that time, I also realized that I had put football first in my life instead of placing God on the throne.

Whatever you meditate on over and over, that's your religion. At that point in my life, my thoughts were all about football—not God. I knew I needed to change, to get back to the foundation of my faith. I recognized I needed to surrender everything to God because football wasn't going to last forever.

Jordan (87) making a touchdown catch for Vanderbilt while being defended by Florida's Cody Riggs

›› Mark Humphrey/AP/Shutterstock

Since giving control of my life over to Christ, the game no longer consumes me. That doesn't mean I don't care about football. I do! But it means I can be the same person in all situations. Before a game or after a game, after a win or after a loss, I am joyful. Even through injury and trials, I have peace. I can be open to my family and friends. Ultimately, I know this strength and peace only comes from Christ.

As a Christian, I'm a servant to people. God calls all his followers to serve, and he gives us plenty of role models in the Bible. The apostle Paul started off many of his letters in the New Testament with a phrase describing himself as a "servant of God." He used that phrase as his title. Paul didn't give his opinions, he just relayed the messages his Master wanted him to convey.

SLAY **THE** GIANTS

My faith in God is straightforward and no nonsense. Maybe that's why my favorite Bible verse is 1 Samuel 17:48 (NLT). It simply says, "As Goliath moved closer to attack, David quickly ran out to meet him." When you read about David, you realize he did two things exceedingly well. First, he did his job tending sheep. Second, he loved the Lord. So when the moment came for him to display his faith in God, David *ran* at Goliath. This Goliath dude was huge and wore all kinds of armor. He was the original alpha male! He was a giant every man feared. But David had no fear of him because David was filled with the Holy Spirit.

When I think about that verse, I often ask myself a question: *Do I run that quickly, without hesitation, when God calls me?* David didn't stop and ask anyone's opinion of what he should do. God called him to action, and he ran into action. David didn't have an identity crisis. He knew who he was and whose he was. We need to have the faith that David displayed. We need to boldly slay the giants in our lives.

That's what I strive to be—a messenger of God's love to believers and non-believers alike. I want to serve everyone, but I only answer to One. It's that mindset that's helped me take the pressure off. I don't have to worry about other people's opinions. If I'm being criticized in the media or by fans or on social media, I can let it go. I don't have to try and be perfect. I know I'll never be! We all sin and fall short. I don't have to be perfect to get to God; God was perfect and he came to me.

One of the biggest lies that the world will tell you is to love yourself. In the book of Matthew, when the Pharisees tried to trick Jesus on a legal issue, Jesus told them the first and greatest commandment of the Law: "Love the Lord your God with all your heart and with all your soul and with all your mind [. . .] Love your neighbor as yourself" (Matthew 22:37–39). The message Jesus is giving here is that if you love God fully and love your neighbor, you will naturally and automatically love

Jordan (87) while playing for the Bills, a year after leaving Philadelphia
›› AP/Shutterstock

yourself. You don't have to try and love yourself, because God's got you. Don't have an identity crisis and focus on loving yourself. Trust that if you love God and love others, he's going to take care of you.

That's my best advice. When you tap into an eternal source and stop worrying about everything that is temporary, you'll discover your true identity.

CHAPTER 16

ALFRED MORRIS
Man on Fire

@FredoSauce Man, it funny how we met! We had played against each other in the past. But I didn't think we would have our first conversation through gymnastics. Haha! Naw, but bro you're an AWESOME man of faith! Thank you for being a bright light in the world. Keeping being GREAT bro! #salute #faithfulseasons #teammorris

Florida Atlantic University	Pensacola, FL	Running Back

Sportswriters have described NFL running back Alfred Morris as a "proverbial smiley face emoji" when he's *not* on the field. He's known throughout the league as being humble and polite.

On the field, Alfred is a fierce competitor. After being taken in the sixth round of the 2012 NFL Draft by Washington, his impressive training camp and preseason performances earned him the starting job as a rookie. Alfred enjoyed four years as the Redskins' starter, racking up one-thousand-yard performances during his first three seasons in the league. In 2016, Dallas signed the powerful back. At 5'10" inches and 220 pounds, Alfred runs hard! 2016 was the same year the Cowboys drafted Ezekiel Elliott in the first round. With Elliott getting most of the carries that year, Alfred took on a backup role. That role changed in 2017 when Elliott had to sit out several games on suspension. Alfred immediately made his presence felt by rushing for 127 yards against his former team on November 30, helping the Cowboys to a 38–14 win over the Redskins.

Through his first six NFL seasons, Alfred rushed for more than 5,500 yards—averaging an impressive 4.4 yards a carry! His play on the field earned him two Pro Bowl appearances (2013 and 2014) and second-team All-Pro honors in 2012. As much as Alfred appreciates his offensive linemen opening holes for him

Alfred (center) running the ball for the Cowboys
›› Eric Risberg/AP/Shutterstock

to run, he appreciates even more what Jesus did to open the door for him to succeed in the NFL while opening the doors to heaven for him in eternity.

I worshiped an idol in high school. It wasn't football. It wasn't fame. It was a girl I dated. I did everything for her and constantly thought about her. I put her before myself, which isn't necessarily a bad thing. But I also put her before the Lord. After dating her in high school and into college, I realized I was idolizing her.

At the same time, I knew God's Word said not to have idols in our lives. I'd grown up in a churchgoing household where my parents instilled in me very positive values and life morals. My father taught me and my six brothers how to treat women properly and how to be gentlemen. My mother did everything for us, while also obtaining four college degrees. It was my parents who started my foundation in Christ. Through their guidance and example, I came to Christ at a young age.

While I knew the truth, I didn't always follow it. Looking back, I was "lukewarm" about my faith and easily led astray. My relationship with this girl came to a point where I knew it needed to end. It was too toxic.

LIFTED **UP**

I love Scripture! It is the true Word of God, and his Word is everything. My life motto is represented in my favorite Bible verse from James 4:6: "But he gives us more grace. That is why Scripture says: 'God opposes the proud but shows favor to the humble.'" I believe that if we humble ourselves, God will exalt us. It is programmed in me to consistently humble myself in every situation that tests me. I have been overlooked many times throughout my life, from playing football in high school and not making the all-star list to becoming a northwest Florida MVP. From going to college and being benched as a fullback to becoming the star running back. And from finally making it to the NFL, where I wasn't even expected to make the team, to starting every single game for four years. No matter how many times man may overlook or doubt me, God always has a plan for me.

But it was still hard to come to terms with the decision to end it and I kept putting it off. Then one night I was in my room, breaking down with tears in my eyes, and the only person I could lean on was God. I prayed to him to guide me through this tough situation. I asked him to help me follow through on the decision that I needed to make. In that moment, I realized I no longer wanted to be lukewarm; I wanted to be on fire for the Lord. I committed right then and there to stay on fire for him from that point on.

Being a Christian is something that gets thrown around often. I compare it to using the word *love*. Most people will say that they "love" someone but not truly act in a loving way toward that person. Claiming to be a Christian is more than words. To be a Christ follower means you walk the walk and talk the talk. You cannot be half in. My faith in Christ trumps everything else in my life. It trumps being an NFL player. It trumps being a husband, father, or son. It is a lifestyle to me. I don't say I am a Christian just to say it. I live it.

My faith has been my saving grace throughout my football career. All the way back to high school, I was always the underdog. To achieve my dreams, I had to stand firm in my faith and keep pushing.

MY FAITH HAS BEEN MY SAVING GRACE THROUGHOUT MY FOOTBALL CAREER.

During my senior year at Pine Forest High School in Pensacola, Florida, I rushed for 1,049 yards with seventeen touchdowns. Like most high school teams, we played both sides of the ball. On defense, I added 147 tackles and five interceptions. College scouts started making trips to my school and pitching very nice offers. At first, I was confused on where I should go. I consulted with my mother, and she told me to pray about it. I did just that and decided to commit to Florida Atlantic University.

SOARING WITH THE OWLS

Football earned me a scholarship to attend FAU, but I was also serious about my studies. When I graduated in 2012, I became the first one of my siblings to graduate from college. It was a huge achievement for me and my family.

Alfred (with ball) runs for a first down past Daniel White during a game between FAU and UAB

›› Butch Dill/AP Images

I was also achieving big things on the football field. After seeing little action as a freshman, my offensive role expanded. In my final three years as an Owl, I rushed for more than 3,500 yards and scored twenty-eight touchdowns.

Following college, the Washington Redskins selected me in the sixth round of the NFL Draft. For the first four years of my career, I started every game. The hardest transition came when I joined the Dallas Cowboys in 2016. Instead of being the featured back, I was placed on the bench behind rookie Ezekiel Elliott. Zeke had a monster year, gaining more than 1,600 yards. But one player's success often means less opportunities for others. I started to doubt myself. *Why was this happening to me?* I wondered. For the first time in my professional football career, I was put on the inactive list, which meant I didn't suit up for a game.

Though it was a very low point in my life, I held the Lord high. I became closer to God and strengthened my relationship with him. Sometimes when you're in the eye of the storm, it's hard to see a way out. It can be very easy to think negatively. Instead of giving in to the darkness, I strived to look to the light. By looking to God and his Word, he helped me not only get through, but also to become a better husband, father, and player.

God has called all his followers to spread Christ's love to the people we encounter. People need to know that they are loved and that they are sons and daughters of the Most High. I pull my inspiration about love from 1 John 4:7–21, because no matter what you have done in your life or how far you may feel you are from God, he wants a relationship with you. Wherever you are on your spiritual journey, God loves you and he wants to be part of your life. Allow him to "wreck" your life for the better. You won't regret it. When you allow yourself to be truly loved by him, it'll make you on fire about your faith forever.

Alfred (right) taking a handoff from Kirk Cousins while playing for the Washington Redskins

›› Bill Kostroun/AP/Shutterstock

CHAPTER 17

BENJAMIN WATSON
Chasing Perfection

@BenjaminSWatson The journey God has had you on and the lives you have touched is amazing bro. #WPMOY I mean you have so many accomplishments. I can't even keep up . . . you've even been in a movie. Haha (Focus, 2015) I'm just tryin to be like you bro!! On 'n off the field!!

University of Georgia	Norfolk, VA	Tight End

Benjamin Watson always gives 100 percent. His teammates see it every day. And his opponents respect him for it. Just ask the Denver Broncos.

It was the third quarter of a divisional playoff game between the Broncos and the New England Patriots on January 14, 2006. Tom Brady had driven the Patriots to Denver's 5-yard line. New England trailed 10–6 at the time and appeared to be poised for the go-ahead touchdown. But on third down, Denver's All-Pro cornerback Champ Bailey intercepted a Brady pass. Bailey raced out of the end zone with an entourage of blockers flanking him down the field. It looked like a certain pick-six for the Broncos. But from all the way across the field, Benjamin sprinted to close the gap. After running over 100 yards—possibly more if you consider the angle he took—Benjamin blasted into Bailey at the 1-yard line. Both Bailey and the ball flew out of bounds, thwarting a Denver score.

Although this play occurred more than a decade ago, Boston sports-writers still call it one of the greatest plays in Patriots history. The fact that a tight end could run down one of the fastest cornerbacks in the game from the other end of the field is remarkable. And *remarkable* is a perfect word to describe Benjamin Watson.

He entered the league with the Patriots after being selected in the first round of the 2004 NFL Draft. After six years and one Super Bowl victory in New England, Benjamin went to Cleveland, where he led the Browns in receptions, receiving yards, and receiving touchdowns in 2010. In 2013, he joined the New Orleans Saints. Benjamin enjoyed three years with the Saints, including a career-high seventy-four catches for 825 yards in 2015—his twelfth season in the league! Following a year in Baltimore, Benjamin is back in New Orleans for the 2018 season.

Benjamin has always been a brilliant and gifted athlete. His score of 48 on the Wonderlic Test (the third-highest in NFL history) and 4.4 second 40-yard dash prove that fact. But it's his never-give-up attitude and 100 percent effort that make him stand apart. Those characteristics are obvious on the field and in his walk with the Lord.

I learned the importance of giving 100 percent from my parents. My father used to say, "If you're going to be a bank robber, I want you to be the best bank robber ever."

Of course, he didn't want me to become a bank robber. My dad was a pastor. But his point was that he wanted me to be good at whatever I chose to do, and to work hard at it as unto the Lord.

That was my dad's message to me and my five younger siblings. My parents taught us right from wrong and to live out our beliefs. My parents weren't perfect—no parents are—but they had integrity, demonstrated to us what a loving marriage looks like, lived their beliefs, and taught us to care for others.

We attended church every Sunday, went to youth camps, and participated in vacation Bible school. We knew the Bible and memorized Scripture. So even at a young age, I understood that knowing *about* God was not the same as *knowing* God. When I was about six years old, I asked Jesus to come into my life.

I remember the exact evening. My father was a pastor, but he had also played football at the University of Maryland. When I was little, he would try to toughen me up. During our time together, before I went to bed each night, he would hold this big teddy bear for me to fight. One night I lost the tussle with the bear and called for my father to bring the bear back for another fight. I fought the teddy bear again and won. Then my father shared John 3:16 with me: "For God so loved the world that he gave his one and only Son, that whoever believes in him shall not perish but have eternal life." He asked me what would happen when I died. Even at that age, I understood that sin separated me from God. The only way to salvation was to accept Jesus Christ as my Savior. That night, I knelt beside my father and prayed to ask Jesus to forgive my sins and be my Lord.

FOOTBALL AND FAITH

My faith was a huge part of my life growing up, and so was football. I helped lead Northwestern High School in Rock Hill, South Carolina, to a state championship during my junior year. And as a senior, I caught thirty-one passes for 515 yards to earn a second-consecutive All-Region selection.

Initially, I attended Duke University and played football. But then I transferred to the University of Georgia. In three seasons with the Bulldogs, I caught sixty-five passes for more than 850 yards, and scored six touchdowns.

In 2004, I was drafted by New England. The Patriots had become the most successful team in the NFL, primarily due to their rigidly demanding processes. Under this system, players were berated for mistakes. While I knew the coaches were correcting me to make me a better player, I didn't always accept it that way. I began to struggle with perfectionism. When I did anything less than perfect, I felt tremendous guilt for being a failure. Your conscience should prick you when you do something wrong, but I went beyond those pricks and wouldn't give myself any breaks.

Benjamin (right) catches a touchdown pass by jumping over Sammy Knight during the 2008 AFC Divisional Playoff game
>> Matt Campbell/EPA/Shutterstock

By my fifth season in the league, my perfectionism had expanded from the football field into my personal and spiritual life. Not only would I get down on myself if I dropped a pass, missed a blocking assignment, or ran the wrong route, I began to tie my self-worth to what I did rather than to who I was.

It was then that I consulted with my father about my troubles. My father was, and still is, my hero. As a pastor, people looked up to him. He was larger than life. At this point, with all the mistakes I was making on the field, I felt that I wasn't measuring up to being his son. My father helped me see the error of that thinking. I didn't have to earn God's grace—or even my place in the Watson family. Unconditional love from my heavenly Father and my earthly father already had that covered.

Benjamin with his family

>> Photo courtesy of Benjamin Watson

Before I spoke to my father, I was in bondage. I had a faulty understanding of salvation, and I was trying to earn God's favor and the approval of others. Ephesians 2:8–9 clarified things for me. These two verses helped me see that I needed to give God control of ALL circumstances in my life. Salvation was a gift—it couldn't be earned through trying to please others. This understanding gave me the freedom to fail. I didn't have to worry about messing up, so I started to play better. It's amazing how far God can take you when you aren't trying to do it all by yourself.

Benjamin speaking out about his faith at a March for Life event

>> Cheriss May/NurPhoto via Getty Images

The freedom I've found on the field and in my life through this understanding is something I want everyone to experience. My best football occurred *after* coming to this realization—you have worth before God that outshines anything the world can provide! It doesn't matter how you grew up. I was a pastor's kid. But your family life has no bearing on who you are before God. God doesn't show favoritism based on your outward appearance, the color of your skin, or your financial wealth. God only looks at your heart. No matter what your circumstances, God loves you and he sent his son to die for you.

I'll never be perfect. That doesn't mean I don't try to live like Christ every day. I do. And I fail. I fail on the football field. I fail in my role as a husband and a father. That's why integrity and honesty are so important; so is asking for forgiveness when you're wrong. We can never be perfect on our own. But the Bible tells us to keep pressing on, to take hold of the perfection that's found in Christ. Only in him and through his power can we be made perfect.

BOAST **IN THE** LORD

My favorite Bible verse changes depending upon the circumstances in my life. But Jeremiah 9:23–24 is an all-timer: "Let not the wise boast of their wisdom or the strong boast of their strength or the rich boast of their riches, but let the one who boasts boast about this: that they have the understanding to know me, that I am the Lord, who exercises kindness, justice and righteousness on earth, for in these I delight." I want to delight in the same things that God delights in, so my family and I want to support things that promote kindness, justice, and righteousness. I'd like to be known for that.

CHAPTER 18

TYLER PATMON
Lionhearted

@Lion_hearted_26 T-Pat my dog 4life. We been cool since college, train together, compete against each other, and push each other to be GREAT. Keep God 1st always bro! We next up! #RealTruth #lionhearted #StrapHaus

University of Kansas/Oklahoma State University	Round Rock, TX	Cornerback

Dallas Pro Bowl receiver Dez Bryant lined up for a one-on-one route drill early in the Cowboys' 2015 training camp. A few months prior, the receiver had signed a five-year, $70 million contract. Second-year cornerback Tyler Patmon took his spot, facing the superstar two yards off the line of scrimmage. Dez was determined to show that he had not lost his intensity since signing a new contract. Tyler was determined to keep his spot on the team and show he could lock down any receiver in the NFL.

At the snap of the ball, Tyler jammed Dez within the five-yard zone. Dez's helmet flew off. In retaliation, Dez slapped off Tyler's helmet. Punches were thrown as teammates scrambled to break up the fight. Moments later, the two men hugged it out.

"You don't want someone weak on your team," Dez said to reporters after practice. "Patmon was undrafted, and he's fighting for respect. He's got mine. I'll go to war with a guy like that any day of the week."

Dez saw what others already knew . . . Tyler Patmon wasn't backing down from anyone.

Coming up as a young kid, I always noticed my family didn't have very much money. I wanted to change that. I told my grandma I was going to take care of her and "buy her the city."

Seeing your family struggle can do two things to you: motivate you or put you in a slump. For me, it was motivation. It created a drive in me to be great. It gave me an anger. The anger showed itself whenever my team lost. Losing was not something I took well. Pretty soon, opponents and even my teammates started describing me as a hothead, as someone who always wanted to fight.

LOSING WAS NOT SOMETHING I TOOK WELL.

Proverbs 29:11 says, "Fools give full vent to their rage." Looking back, I acted foolish. But at the time, I didn't know any better. I didn't know Christ as my Savior or read the Bible. I thought my anger gave me strength. Now I realize it made it more difficult to accomplish my goals.

I always dominated my friends at sports. When I began playing organized football for the first time in sixth grade, I knew I'd found my ticket out. I was a natural. But youth football in Texas is competitive and tough. Midway through a middle school season, I fractured my fibula and tibia right above my ankle. I didn't realize how badly I was injured when it happened. But when I tried to stand up, I couldn't. I rolled over and looked at my leg. It was shaped like the letter *V*.

That ended my season. I'd find myself discouraged at times, but it didn't end my dream. If anything, it just stoked the fire. My pops and I rehabbed my leg until I was good enough to play again. Going into high school, I was excited to get back on the field and prove myself. Back then, it was all about me. *I* needed to prove myself, make a name for myself, and catch the attention of colleges.

Tyler during his early football years, alongside his dad

›› Photo courtesy of Tyler Patmon

As a freshman, I dominated the older guys. But once again, an injury took me out for the year. This time I dislocated and chipped my elbow. More pain, more rehab.

When I got back on the field this time, I became a dominating cornerback for Vista Ridge High School in Cedar Park, Texas. Recruiters started to take notice. More than a million students play high school football. Of that massive number, only about 3,500 earn a star rating. I became a three-star recruit. Only about thirty guys were tagged as five-star recruits. Being a three-star put me in the top two thousand football players in the nation. Immediately, schools started contacting me. After receiving an offer from the University of Kansas, I committed early in my junior year.

Going into my senior season, I was more confident than ever. I knew what my future held, and I was playing on another level. But during our fourth game, I tore a piece of cartilage in my right shoulder. Even more pain and more rehab. But even worse, I worried that Kansas might take away its scholarship offer. By this time, however, I knew how to work through injuries. So I rehabbed my shoulder and walked onto the Jayhawks campus fully healthy.

After redshirting my first year, I began playing cornerback at Kansas. Seasons were tough. We didn't win a lot of games. Injuries plagued me. I tore a muscle in my upper leg and also tore some cartilage in my knee. Coaches seemed to change every year. Each coaching change meant a new system, which meant more learning and having to prove myself all over again.

I managed to stay on the field, but injuries limited my level of play. One of the hardest things as an athlete is knowing your potential and not being able to reach it. I knew I was capable of performing better, and my frustration started to turn into anger. My anger began to show itself on the field and in the locker room. I believed I wasn't being given the recognition I deserved. I was also angry because of the injuries.

THE PROBLEMS IN MY LIFE WERE OFTEN CAUSED OR MADE WORSE BY THE FACT I DIDN'T RESPOND THE RIGHT WAY.

Nobody likes an angry teammate. Coaches don't like angry players. They can bring dissention to a team instead of unity. In December 2012, after another injury-plagued year, I got a message from our head coach. His words were clear: "I think it's time for you to move on from the University of Kansas." After three seasons, I'd been kicked off the football team.

The coach's message shocked and hurt me. I had no idea what was going to happen next. I was confused, and now angry at the world. But the coach's decision forced me to examine myself and my lifestyle. I really began to look at myself in the mirror. I saw how the problems in my life were often caused or made worse by the fact I didn't respond the right way. I began to look to God for answers. God started showing me, "You reap what you sow."

FROM COWBOY TO COWBOYS

God took care of me during that time. He gave me the opportunity to attend Oklahoma State University. The Cowboys' football program was more successful and nationally respected than Kansas' program was. I knew it was a great opportunity and that God had gotten me there. I began to make a shift. I tried to better myself. The problem was, I was trying to bring myself up to God's level and prove I was worthy. That was impossible. God had come down to my level already. He'd loved me while I was still a sinner. I couldn't "fix" myself through my own efforts. But my efforts were keeping God from reaching me.

MY EFFORTS WERE KEEPING GOD FROM REACHING ME.

Thankfully, God intervened. My uncle was a preacher. So, during a conversation, he asked me if I'd given my life to Christ. I didn't really know what that meant. My uncle explained the path to salvation, something I'd never had explained to me before. He told me that I needed to trust God as my Savior and allow him to change me from the inside. I couldn't earn salvation; God gave it as a gift through his son, Jesus. That was when I made a life-changing decision. On April 21, 2014, I chose to follow God with my life.

I had a successful season at Oklahoma State. During my senior year, I played in ten games, made thirty tackles, grabbed an interception, and forced and recovered a fumble. I knew I had the skills to play in the NFL. Though during the draft season, I didn't receive an invitation to the NFL Combine. No agents called. No articles were written about me in draft reports. Nothing. I was a nobody to the NFL.

A LION'S AMBITION

Oklahoma State put on a Pro Day for NFL scouts. I performed well and caught the attention of a few teams. I received some calls a few weeks before the draft and got an agent. So, when draft day came, I was excited. I watched the entire thing—from the first round to the seventh round. Justin Gilbert, who played opposite of me at Oklahoma State, was the first cornerback drafted. He went eighth overall in the first round, to Cleveland. I saw other cornerbacks go. I knew I was better than some of those guys. In all, thirty-five cornerbacks were drafted. I wasn't one of them. I felt crushed. I literally cried my heart out. Then players started signing as undrafted free agents. My friends were getting deals. But still no call.

Finally, my phone rang. It was my agent, calling to tell me that no team wanted to sign me. He said he'd keep making phone calls. I thought my dream was dead. But after reaching out to a few teams, my agent called back and said I could get a tryout with the Dallas Cowboys or Miami Dolphins. Rarely does a player make the NFL from just a tryout. Teams have already put money into their draft picks and free agents. But at least now I had a shot.

Growing up in Texas, I showed up at the Cowboys tryout on full charge. Fourteen other players were there too. I put everything I had into those two days, and they were two of the best days I'd ever had as a football player.

Tyler (20) returning an interception for a touchdown against the Arizona Cardinals

» James D. Smith/AP Images

I walked into the tryout as a long shot, I walked out signed as a free agent. The signing didn't guarantee me a spot on the team, but it meant the Cowboys wanted to see more of me at training camp. I was sore all over, but it was one of my proudest moments as a player.

When I came to training camp, my motivation was off the charts. Nobody could tell me no. I fought hard in every drill. I studied defensive schemes. I put maximum effort into everything I did. During our third preseason game against the Miami Dolphins, I flew all over the field. I had two interceptions, including one I returned for a touchdown, I forced a fumble, and I made six tackles. By the end of the preseason, my dream had come true. I'd made the fifty-three-man roster of the Dallas Cowboys.

But you can never be satisfied in the NFL. You have to keep pushing. Going into my second year at Dallas, our nickelback tore his knee. I was the next man up. A nickelback is usually the fifth defensive back to come on the field in certain defensive packages, added to the base defense that consists of two cornerbacks and two safeties. Even though nickelback was sort of a new position for me, I was happy to be that fifth guy.

From the start of the season, however, my body hadn't felt right. I fought through and led the team in pass breakups. But I was also making mistakes—too many. I was learning as I went. Then I got benched.

It was one of the hardest moments in my professional life. I felt betrayed. I took it as a personal insult instead of as a professional decision. The coaches had a more experienced player they wanted to give a chance at nickel. I should've understood that. Instead, my pride got in the way. My anger came out. Basically, I handled the situation completely wrong.

CONFIDENCE **FROM** CHRIST

My favorite Scripture was written by David and speaks about not being afraid. It's Psalm 27:1–4. The first three verses of that passage say: "The Lord is my light and my salvation—whom shall I fear? The Lord is the stronghold of my life—of whom shall I be afraid? When the wicked advance against me to devour me, it is my enemies and my foes who will stumble and fall. Though an army besiege me, my heart will not fear; though war break out against me, even then I will be confident."

When I gave my life to the Lord, I stopped trying to fit in with the world. Now I only want to fit in with God. These verses give me the strength and confidence to do the right things rather than to follow the crowd. It's easy to do what everyone else does, but it takes courage to go in a different direction. Don't be afraid to stick out for God. When you're following him, there's nothing to fear.

I stopped talking to teammates and coaches. I focused only on myself. I just cared about my job—not what was best for the team—and I was definitely not trying to act like a godly man. The Cowboys ended up releasing me. After playing twenty-two games for Dallas over two seasons, I no longer had a job.

It took more than a year before I could look back at this situation and realize how badly I'd responded. I sat on the couch for a year. No NFL team gave me a chance. From the outside, it looked like a terrible time in my life, but it ended up being one of the best. This was my turning point—my REAL turning point. Being cut brought me closer to God. I began to see that God was in control. He wouldn't allow me to fail. I became a better man and a better Christian because of the situation.

From then on, I changed the way I acted toward people on and off the field. With God as the driving force in my life, I carried myself in a godly manner. I corrected myself when I responded badly. I apologized to people if I became angry. God was my number one priority. I saw him at work in my daily life. And I saw him open the door that let me get my feet back in the NFL.

> **I BEGAN TO SEE THAT GOD WAS IN CONTROL. HE WOULDN'T ALLOW ME TO FAIL.**

In late 2015, I signed with the Miami Dolphins. I only played two games for the them before being released again. Injuries kept plaguing me, but I didn't give up. During the 2016 season, I was signed and released by the Tennessee Titans, the Kansas City Chiefs, and the Carolina Panthers.

Then in 2017, I got another tryout and became a Jacksonville Jaguar. I appeared in thirteen games for the Jaguars. It was awesome being on a team that was having a breakthrough season. I will never forget what

God has done for me in my good times and bad. He showed me my true character. He also showed me how I had to change my ways in order to walk with him. I know I'm walking toward my true destiny now. Nothing the world throws at me can alter who I am, because God is my rock. His strength is all I need. Because of him, I'll never quit. And that's the true meaning of being lionhearted!

Tyler (wearing 37) tackling Mike Evans during his first year as a Jaguar

›› AP/Shutterstock

CHAPTER 19

AP/Shutterstock

DAVID BASS

Keep Faith & Trust the Process

@dbass91 Man when is the next time we going to Monell's. Haha . . . naw, bro I'm glad we met in Tennessee. It was a tough year but you just gotta roll wit da punches. Keep fighting bro, we will look back on our careers one day and it will all be worth it! Fo' real though, when we hittin Monell's!!!!!!?? Best soul food in Nashville—oooooweee!

| Missouri Western State University | St. Louis, MO | Linebacker |

David Bass graduated as the all-time sacks leader at Missouri Western State University. Never heard of it? Neither had a lot of NFL scouts. David started fifty games for the Division II Griffons and finished with more than forty sacks! Averaging nearly one sack a game would normally secure a top spot for a defensive lineman in the NFL Draft. But NFL scouts weren't convinced the 6'4", 267-pound defender could compete at the next level.

David would have to earn his spot in the NFL. The average length of a defensive lineman's career is three years. However, he's played twice that long. So far in his career, David's taken the field in more than sixty games and sacked some NFL greats, including Matthew Stafford and Drew Brees. Teammates say that he goes onto the field and does the work. And it's certainly taken a lot of work and faith to help David achieve the dream of playing in the NFL.

———————

I'm not an offensive lineman. My high school football coach at University City High in Missouri thought otherwise. The reason was, I was pretty big for my age. But while I had good size for my school, I was small for the position and definitely smaller than the players I was trying to block. I remember getting frustrated a lot and feeling like a failure. Every time I would mess up or miss a block, I would question myself: *What am I doing here?* That's what ultimately led me to quit the football team.

Fortunately, my mom and my coach convinced me to get back on the team. I did, and I made it through the season. Then my school had a coaching change, which meant big changes for me too. The new coach wanted me to play defensive end and tight end. Now those positions fit my size and skills way better! That's when I began to flourish on the field and started to see my future in football.

THROUGH THE VALLEY

Sometimes it can seem that no matter what you do, you don't get any breaks. A coach may have you in the wrong position. You might feel stuck on the bench. You give your all, but you receive no respect. I'm here to tell you to keep going, trust the process, and, most importantly, don't give up! The circumstances you go through help you become the person that God

David with his dad

▶▶ Photo courtesy of David Bass

David and his mom today

▶▶ Photo courtesy of David Bass

wants you to be. Keep your faith! I'm definitely glad I did, because there were plenty of times where I could've quit for good.

My dad passed away when I was only seven years old. It hurt a lot! He was an accomplished athlete in his own right, especially on the basketball court. Growing up, my mom raised me and my little brother, Darrian, right outside of St. Louis. My mom always encouraged me to live the productive life my dad hoped I would have. If he was still here, I think he would be proud of me and my brother. We've both come a long way.

Baseball was huge in St. Louis when I was young. Still is. I played every sport, but baseball was my first love. I used to love blasting the ball from home plate into the outfield. But as I got older, the sport's slow pace caused me to pursue other interests, especially football and basketball.

Once I got moved to defensive end on the high school football team, I made enough big plays that colleges took notice. I started getting scholarship offers from Division II and NAIA schools, but no Division I universities. My skills on the basketball court got me some me offers to hoop at the Division I level, but I felt like football gave me the best opportunity to make a career out of it. I chose to attend Missouri Western State University and play football. It was close to home, and they offered me a full-ride scholarship.

David (91) tracking down Christine Michael
during the East-West Shrine Classic game

>> Chris O'Meara/AP/Shutterstock

As soon as I got there, I started thriving with the Griffons. I avoided injuries, thank God, and started in fifty straight games. I felt like I did everything I could to catch the eye of NFL scouts, but it seemed like many of them had a preconceived notion that players in the Mid-America Intercollegiate Athletic Association were inferior. I mean, it wasn't the SEC. But I was ballin'. My teammates and the athletes I lined up against understood the game and worked just as hard as anyone else. Sometimes I couldn't understand why we didn't get any respect. Nevertheless, during my senior year, I ended up being a finalist for the Gene Upshaw Award. It's an award that goes to the top Division II lineman in the nation. I also got to showcase my talents in the East-West Shrine Game.

When I entered the 2013 NFL Draft, I hoped my performance on the field would speak for itself, yet I wasn't sure I'd be selected. Then, in the seventh round, the Oakland Raiders called my name. Man, it was so dope! I was only the third player ever from Missouri Western State University to be taken in the draft!

CHANGES FOR THE GOOD

Not only was I looking forward to a new opportunity in the NFL, I was enjoying my new life in Christ. I had accepted Jesus as my Savior in March of 2012. And I'd already seen God's work on my heart.

While I was growing up, I'd find myself focusing on the other defensive ends and players on the team. If there were four of us competing for two starting spots, I'd hope they did poorly in the drills so I'd win the job. But now I wanted all the players to perform to the best of their abilities and to stay healthy. It was a total change in my attitude. My faith was in God, not my own abilities or luck.

MY FAITH WAS IN GOD, NOT MY OWN ABILITIES OR LUCK.

I optimistically started training camp with the Raiders. But pretty soon I began to wonder if some NFL scouts were right: *Maybe players from small colleges can't keep up with the speed of the NFL.* For some reason, I just couldn't get to the quarterback like I did in college. I specifically remember this one play in practice. Let me walk you through it. I lined up in a position called the 7-technique, between the tight end and offensive tackle. I had a good stance. The ball got snapped, and I took off. But the offensive lineman and tight end I lined up against pancaked me so bad. I ended up flat on my back, looking at the sky. *Aghhhh,* that was tough.

But instead of dwelling on the negative thoughts and the bad plays, which can be easy to do, I pushed them away and fought through all my adversity. I worked hard every practice, made adjustments, and eventually improved my play. It wasn't enough.

At the end of training camp, the Raiders released me. Being released by an NFL team can really shake your faith. I wondered why God had even brought me that far only to fall short. I was disappointed and angry. I found myself bitter at Oakland and secretly hoping they'd have a terrible season.

PLAY **FOR THE** LORD

My all-time favorite verse in the Bible is Colossians 3:23–24: "Whatever you do, work at it with all your heart, as working for the Lord, not for human masters, since you know that you will receive an inheritance from the Lord as a reward. It is the Lord Christ you are serving." This verse inspires me not to worry about other people's opinions. I'm only concerned with what God wants me to do. I'm working for a heavenly inheritance, not earthly riches. If I give everything I have on the field to glorify him, I know he'll guide my life. And the more I give, the more I've seen given back to me.

But as I had time to reflect and give the situation to God, I was reminded that he had a plan for my life. I knew nothing happened beyond his control, and he could use all my circumstances for his glory. So I chose to stay faithful to God, and, honestly, he has blessed me with more than I could ever ask for.

David in his first season with the Jets

>> Chris Szagola/CSM/Shutterstock

Although the Raiders had released me, the Chicago Bears quickly gave me a spot on their fifty-three-man roster. I was excited to go back to the middle of the country and be closer to my family. I immersed myself in Chicago. I did a lot of charitable events and gave back to the fans in any way I could. But after two enjoyable seasons with the Bears, I was cut again. This time Tennessee picked me up. I ended up starting for the Titans during seven games in the 2015 season and played thirteen games for Tennessee in 2016.

Life in the NFL is exciting. But it can also be filled with doubts. *Am I good enough? Will I get signed again? What will the next move mean?* Ever since accepting Christ, I've seen clear changes in how I deal with difficulties and make it through life. I pray several times a day. I read my Bible daily and really enjoy learning about God. Plus, my phone is now filled with Christian music that helps lift my spirit whenever I get down. I love worship, listening to other people's testimonies, and hearing pastors explain the gospel. I know I'll never fully understand God. But I want to build a personal relationship with Jesus Christ, who died for my sins. That's my advice to everyone. Do the right things for the right reason, and not only will you be a better person, you'll also make others around you better.

DO THE RIGHT THINGS FOR THE RIGHT REASON.

Speaking of better, I feel like I keep learning more and getting better on the field. After the Titans let me go, I was signed by the Seattle Seahawks in 2017. I only played a few games with the Seahawks, but it was amazing to be on such a dominating defense. They released me on September 19, and two days later I was playing for another dominating defense in New York. I ended up having one of my best seasons for the Jets—3.5 sacks in thirteen games. As the 2018 season starts, I'm excited because my little brother, Darrian, has been invited to Jets camp. This could be the break he needs.

You may feel that you don't get many breaks in life. That's how I felt in high school and plenty other times during my life. But I hope my story can help you. We are all different, but I know if you put your faith in God and trust in his process, you will win every time!

David (standing) and his brother at the gym
>> Photo courtesy of David Bass

CHAPTER 20

MANNY RAMIREZ

No Pain, No Gain

@Manny63ramierez I met you during my rookie year with the Denver Broncos. Our meeting was not a pleasant one either. Haha! Found out you a beast of a blocker!! But, off the field, you one of the most chill dudes I have ever met. Thank you for being a role model bro!! #mmgfit

Texas Tech	Houston, TX	Offensive Lineman/Center

It's a play Manny Ramirez would like to forget. But thanks to YouTube, it'll never go away.

Denver Broncos lineman Manny Ramirez readied himself to snap the ball for the first offensive play in Super Bowl XLVIII. Seattle fans, as they're known to do, roared from the stands. Broncos quarterback Peyton Manning barked out the signals from the shotgun position. The ball was supposed to be snapped on a certain cadence, but Manny, who was playing center, couldn't hear it. Peyton started walking toward the line of scrimmage just as Manny hiked it. The ball sailed over Peyton's head and into the end zone. The Broncos recovered, giving the Seahawks two points for a safety.

After the game, Peyton said the play was "nobody's fault." But Manny took full responsibility for the botched snap.

While that one play may live forever, what's forgotten are the thousands of plays where Manny made the pass block, had the perfect snap, or opened the hole for a big gain. Throughout his nine-year NFL career, Manny played in eighty-three games for some of the top offenses in the league. But a freak bar fight in college almost ended Manny's career before it began.

It was a hot and humid night in Lubbock, Texas. I'd just finished my freshman year at Texas Tech. Some of my friends and teammates wanted to go out to a club right outside of campus. I really didn't want to go, but I gave in, telling myself that a "good team player" would go along for the sake of team building.

Looking back, I should've gone with my first instinct and stayed home. A fight broke out at the club, and I stepped in to protect some of my smaller teammates. I may have been a freshman, but I stood 6'3" and weighed 325 pounds. I thought my size—and the fact that I could bench press more than 500 pounds—would put a stop to the situation. It didn't. I was jumped from behind and was hit in the face and head with beer bottles and bar stools. I suffered a severe gash across my lip that took sixty stitches to close. At the hospital, the doctor told me that if the cut had been one millimeter higher, a major artery in my face would've been cut. Instead of getting stitches, I would have bled to death between the club and the hospital.

One silly disagreement almost ended my life. I'd gone to college to help my family. My father had suffered a severe heart attack during my junior year of high school. Fortunately, he survived. But as the oldest child, I knew it was my responsibility to care for and support the family if my father could not. After one fight in a bar, I'd come one millimeter from losing it all.

That near-death experience made me realize I lacked something in my life. I'd grown up with a knowledge of who God is and what he can do. But that understanding was all in my head, not in my heart.

God, however, is all-knowing. He knew how to get my attention—through a good woman! One of Texas Tech's head athletic trainers knew a young lady named Iris. He believed she could help me connect with God. The trainer told me that Iris was interested in me. Meanwhile, he told Iris that I was interested in her. We quickly discovered that we'd been deceived, but there was definitely a spark between us and we began to date.

> **THAT NEAR-DEATH EXPERIENCE MADE ME REALIZE I LACKED SOMETHING IN MY LIFE.**

Iris was the daughter of a minister, and from the start she asked me to come to church with her. Other students around campus had asked me to church too. I'd always declined. I said no to her as well. Iris then asked me questions about my beliefs. I had to admit I didn't have a relationship with God. I also said I didn't want to talk about it. Immediately, Iris made it clear that if we couldn't talk together about God, there would be no relationship between us. She wanted a partner in life who would help her grow in her faith. Given that ultimatum, I told her I wasn't the man she was looking for.

We went our separate ways . . . for a while, at least. Eventually, Iris reached out to me again and once more asked me to go to church. I really missed her, so I agreed. She took me to the church where her mother was the pastor. Toward the end of the service, Iris' mom invited anyone who wanted prayer to come to the front of the church. I clung tightly to my seat at the back. Iris went forward. Even at the back of the church, God was convicting me. Suddenly, I felt a warmth rush over me and I began to cry. I told God that I was done doing it my way. I needed his help. I was tired of falling and failing.

I made my way to the front of the church and told the pastor I needed God in my life. Iris was right there. She heard every word. After the service, Iris told me she'd gone to the front of the church and prayed about our relationship. She asked God to give her the wisdom to end it if it wasn't meant to be. But if it was to be, she asked God to please change my heart. Hearing that was proof to me that God works in his time. I've been a believer ever since.

BEST **PLAN**

My favorite verse of the Bible has always been the same, even before I became a Christian. It's Jeremiah 29:11: "'For I know the plans I have for you,' declares the Lord, 'plans to prosper you and not to harm you, plans to give you hope and a future.'" God has his plan set for us, and because of that we will always be okay. Knowing that God's taking care of us should give us comfort. And it's our job to follow through with what God lays in front of us. I know many prayers have been raised to God about me over my lifetime, and those prayers have been answered.

Following that fateful church service, my faith has been my top priority. But when I first returned to football after giving my life to Christ, I struggled with how I should act on the field. I had always been taught that I needed to be physical, dominant, aggressive, and even rude to be successful in football. The goal was complete mental, verbal, and physical domination. As a Christian, some of those tactics conflicted with my beliefs. At first, I thought my faith would make me weaker. But soon I realized I was actually stronger, because I knew God had me covered in spite of what was said or done to me on the football field.

> **I THOUGHT MY FAITH WOULD MAKE ME WEAKER. BUT SOON I REALIZED I WAS ACTUALLY STRONGER.**

MOVING CLOSER TO GOD—LITERALLY

I started nearly fifty games during my college career at Texas Tech, including three bowl games. I was a second-team All-Big 12 offensive lineman selection my junior year and earned honorable mention All-Big 12 honors my senior year. I also set a school record by bench pressing 550 pounds.

The Detroit Lions selected me in the fourth round of the 2007 NFL Draft. I played four years in Detroit before the Broncos signed me in 2011. Moving to the Mile High City helped me grow in my faith. I loved standing with my brother in Christ, teammate Chris Clark, on the sidelines in Denver in our early years. We didn't play much at first. Sometimes we didn't even dress for games. But we stood together and prayed for God's direction in our lives. We asked the Lord for the opportunity to play. Not only did we get that opportunity, we were able to play on the O-line together in the Super Bowl!

While I was growing in my walk with the Lord, I also had some missteps. I remember one game I played for the Broncos where an opponent beat me on a play and I let my temper get the best of me: I swore. On the way from the huddle back to the line of scrimmage, I began apologizing to God out loud and asking his forgiveness. The defensive lineman I was up against thought I was talking to him. He asked what I was saying. I explained the situation to him, and he told me he'd never heard someone apologize like that on the field before. You wouldn't believe some of the conversations we have in the trenches. This was one of the better ones, because God was teaching me to hold my tongue when I got angry.

Another lesson God taught me was that *he* provides all things, not the NFL. My paycheck may have come from an NFL team, but it's God who made that possible. It's no secret that NFL salaries are higher than most jobs.

Manny (63) defends the line against the Denver Broncos while playing for Detroit

>> Duane Burleson/AP/Shutterstock

That's one of the benefits of being the best in the world at a sport. In 2010, after three seasons with the Detroit Lions, I was suddenly released from the team. Then the lockout in 2011 put a tighter grip on our finances. By this time, Iris and I had been married for five years. God spoke to me during that time about who provided me money and security, and it was a good reminder that God was the source of everything I need.

God provided for my family during my career and even after I retired from football in 2016. Later that same year, I took a job as the Director of Player Development at Texas Tech. Going back to my alma mater was a huge honor. So is working with the Red Raiders players to help them develop life skills, take care of their studies, and do community service projects.

Manny (66) gets ready to snap the ball to Peyton Manning during a game against the Jaguars

›› Jack Dempsey/AP/Shutterstock

Over the years, I've adopted my message in life from the example set by a former coach and Seattle Seahawk, the late Dave Brown. I don't want to be a football player who is known as a Christian. I want to be a Christian who happens to be a football player. I'm also not just a Christian when people are watching. It's important to be a Christian when no one is looking. All the challenges in my life have helped me become stronger in my walk with the Lord. And to think, it all started with a wake-up call from a bloodied face. The saying is true: No pain, no gain!

CHAPTER 21

CHRIS CLARK

It's Who You Are, Not What You Do

@clarkboy75 Man, sometimes I wonder what it would have been like if we stayed in Denver. Thank you for encouraging me to keep going in my career bro! From someone who has definitely been through some trials and tribulations and come out on top of it all!! Nothing but love & respect bro! #salute #blessed

| Southern Mississippi University | New Orleans, LA | Offensive Tackle |

You've probably heard of Peyton Manning, one of the best quarterbacks to ever play football. He holds numerous NFL records, including career passing yards (71,940) and passing touchdowns (539). Chris Clark's name, on the other hand, may not sound familiar. That's how it is for offensive linemen. They do the tough work in the trenches without a lot of notoriety. In fact, it's better if an announcer doesn't call their name, because when it happens that usually means they messed up.

At first glance, these two NFL players don't appear to have much in common. But there's more connection between these athletes than first meets the eye. Both were born and raised in New Orleans. Peyton grew up in a wealthy family. Chris grew up in one of the more dangerous parts of the city. Peyton played football from the time he could walk. Chris didn't like football and didn't play the sport seriously until high school. Yet these two players teamed up for one of the most amazing seasons in NFL history. In 2013, Chris started nearly the entire year at left tackle for the Denver Broncos as Peyton set the record for passing touchdowns in a season with fifty-five! Without Chris protecting Peyton's blind side, the potent Broncos offense couldn't have galloped up and down the field. Heading into the 2018 season, Chris has been in the league ten years, playing for Denver, Minnesota, and Houston.

I never wanted to play football. I liked basketball a lot more. But at 6'5" and 315 pounds, I have to admit that I'm better suited for football. And that's just the plan God had for me.

I was raised in a single-parent household as the youngest of eight children. My mother worked three jobs to provide for us. My three older brothers were active in sports, so it wasn't easy feeding all those hungry mouths. I used to watch in amazement as Mom sacrificed for our family. Even today, she's one of my biggest motivators. If she was able to work three jobs to support us, then I have no right to ever be tired! At my size, I should be able to work four jobs if my mother could work three.

Because my mom was out of the house most of the day at one of her jobs, I had a very loose support structure at home. There's an eighteen-year difference between me and my oldest sibling. And because my brothers and sisters had school, sports, and other activities, I was often home alone.

Growing up in New Orleans, there were a lot of ways to get into trouble. I didn't. First, I respected my mother too much. I didn't want to do anything that would cause her grief. Then there was the influence of my seventh-grade teacher, Mr. Tracy Guillory. He showed me what success was. I didn't have my father in my life, and Mr. Guillory taught me what it was to be a man. He taught me how to make a dollar by helping me get several jobs, and he showed me the importance of being accountable for my actions. I owe a lot to him, and we're still close to this day.

As a youngster, I went to church. Well . . . sometimes. I wasn't really paying attention or learning anything, but I felt like it was something I *should* do. God can use a lot of things to get a person's attention and usher them into his kingdom. For me, it was a girl. During my senior year of high school, I met the woman who would one day

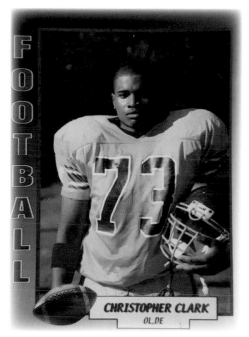

Chris' football card from one of his early teams
>> Photo courtesy of Chris Clark

become my wife. Stacy was a committed Christian. She attended church every Sunday, so I started going too. Soon I gave my life to Christ and had the desire to be in church regularly. As a new Christian, I immersed myself in prayer, read the Bible, and absorbed the teachings of God through sermons.

As my faith grew, so did my vision for God's plan for my life. In my family, it was expected that boys would join the military. That was my plan too. But during my sophomore year of high school, I started to play football. Like I said before, I liked basketball better. And I was good at it: I lettered in basketball and track at McDonogh 35 High School. At first, I struggled on the football field. I didn't know the finer points of football and had a lot to learn. But I've always been a quick learner, and Coach Wayne Reese knew how to develop our football brain. By my senior year, I had offers from more than thirty Division I schools to play football and get a college education.

> **I KNEW GOD HAD GIVEN ME MY SIZE AND ATHLETIC GIFTS FOR A REASON, SO I THOUGHT HE MUST HAVE A PLAN FOR ME.**

I chose to attend Southern Mississippi. From my sophomore year on, I was the starting left tackle. I began earning all-conference honors and getting more exposure nationwide. Going into my senior year, I began to think of the NFL as a career option. After years of being told by naysayers that I wasn't good enough and that I'd never make it, I chose to give football everything I had. I knew God had given me my size and athletic gifts for a reason, so I thought he must have a plan for me that involves this game.

MILE HIGH DREAMS

Even though I believed that football was God's plan for me, making it into the NFL still wasn't easy. I went unclaimed in the 2008 NFL Draft. The Tampa Bay Buccaneers signed me as an undrafted free agent, but released me after the preseason. The Minnesota Vikings picked me up a couple weeks later and put me on their practice squad. Back then, NFL teams were allowed to have eight players on their practice squad. We worked out with the team, did all the same drills, but didn't suit up on Sundays. We were like insurance policies for a team in case a player on the fifty-three-man roster went down with an injury. I was on the Vikings practice squad for two seasons before they cut me loose in in September 2010. One day later, the Denver Broncos picked me up!

The funny thing was that even though I never liked football growing up, when I did allow myself to dream about playing in the league, I always pictured being with the Denver Broncos. I spent the next five seasons in the Mile High City, where I appeared in sixty-nine games, including playing in Super Bowl XLVIII. I'd gone from reluctant lineman to starting left tackle, whose job it was to guard Peyton Manning's blind side on the biggest stage in sports.

Chris (75) protects Peyton Manning against Brian Orakpo
>> Scott Cunningham/Getty Images

GUIDANCE **THROUGH** LIFE'S VALLEYS

Toward the end of my playing time in Denver, I got to sit down with my grandmother and share a moment I'll never forget. My grandmother had thirteen children. I'm one of eight grandkids from just one of her daughters. So, my grandmother has a multitude of grandchildren. Any time I could spend with her was precious. When we talked that day, she told me that Psalm 23 would cover all my needs. Most people know this beautiful chapter of the Bible was written by David. It starts this way: "The Lord is my shepherd, I lack nothing. He makes me lie down in green pastures, he leads me beside quiet waters, he refreshes my soul. He guides me along the right paths for his name's sake. Even though I walk through the darkest valley, I will fear no evil, for you are with me" (verses 1–4).

For me, this passage is a reminder to lean on God for all my needs. I've been through a lot of valleys in life, but I don't fear anything because I know God loves me and guides me.

Although the Seattle Seahawks dominated us in the Super Bowl, winning 43–8, the 2013 season will always be special to me. Our offensive line was ranked third-best in the league by *Pro Football Focus,* a statistical service that analyzes every play of the season. I'd played in all sixteen games and was a starter in fourteen of them. With Peyton posting a record-breaking season, we'd passed the ball a lot. I was on the field for 605 pass-blocking snaps and only allowed thirty-two quarterback pressures. That means about 96 percent of the time I did my job blocking some of the best pass rushers in the game. Stated another way, Peyton only had to hurry his throw in about four of every one hundred passing attempts because my man got around me.

Following five memorable seasons in Denver, the Broncos traded me to Houston in 2015. I played eleven games for the Texans in 2015, all sixteen in 2016 (starting fourteen of them), and ten games in 2017 before an ankle injury ended my season. As a veteran player, I enjoyed teaching the younger players on the team how to handle the pressures of the game. I also tried to pass down the on-field tactics I've learned over the years.

In football you're always one play away from having your career ended. You can't think that way, but it's a reality. Helping others play smart and stay healthy motivates me. I also want to encourage others to follow the plan God has for them. By doing that, they'll become the person God wants them to be. My mother taught

Chris (74) holding back Joey Bosa during a game against the Chargers
›› Bob Levey/Getty Images

me to persevere. Because I didn't quit and followed God, I got to play this game at the highest level. But more than a football player, I am a man of God. It's *who* you are that matters most to God—not what you do.

CHAPTER 22

Nick Wass/AP/Shutterstock

MORGAN COX
Unbelievable

@morgancox46 Man, you are one of the best long snappers in the league. To be honest, I've never seen one like you! Esp one who loves God. It actually amazes me to watch how you carry yourself! Even when Coach was yelling at us in practice, you always seemed so calm. Haha. Keep being the best in the world bro!

University of Tennessee	Collierville, TN	Long Snapper

Through his first eight seasons in the NFL, Morgan Cox has played in exactly 118 games and made exactly *two* tackles. He also has *two* fumble recoveries. Despite these paltry statistics, Morgan is considered one of the best players at his position. In fact, he was named to the Pro Bowl in 2015 and 2016.

Morgan is the long snapper for the Baltimore Ravens. That means he's the player who snaps the ball to the punter and hikes the ball to a holder on a field goal attempt or extra point. He may only be on the field for ten or so plays per game, but his performance can often be the difference between victory and defeat. But the only time announcers pay attention to a long snapper is if the ball is snapped off course. That usually spells disaster for the snapper's team. At these moments, the long snapper gets noticed . . . and booed.

Since Morgan is so good at his job, most people don't know who he is. (Unless you're a Ravens fan, you've probably never heard his name.) But take a moment to think about the difficulty of his very specialized duties. The physical mechanics of long snapping a football aren't simple. You have to spread your feet apart, bend at the waist, and lean over the ball. You peek between your legs to focus on the target. For punts, you're hiking the ball fifteen yards and trying to hit the punter between the waist and chest so he catches the ball perfectly. On field goals, you have to keep the ball low and get it to the holder eight yards behind the line of scrimmage. And you have to get it there fast. The best snappers can zip the ball between their legs at more than fifty miles per hour! Oh, and don't forget that you have a three-hundred-pound lineman trying to knock you over and get to the kicker. So once you launch the ball backward, you have to steady your feet, make a block, and sometimes run down the field to try and make a tackle on a punt. Such is the life of a long snapper . . . a life Morgan Cox always dreamed of.

I became a long snapper in fifth grade. Our coach lined everybody up and gave each of us a shot at long snapping. I wasn't very good at it the first time. My dad and my coach worked with me and I grew into the position. From then on, whenever a football coach would ask who can long snap the ball, I'd raise my hand. There's really no secret to long snapping. It's just a whole lot of hard work and practice.

My grandfather had been a long snapper when he was a kid. He showed me some tips on how to do it. Once he almost knocked me over with the velocity of the ball! I always wanted to be like him. My grandfather was a building contractor and often took me to the job site with him. He never missed any athletic event that I, or any of his other grandchildren, participated in. He lived with Parkinson's disease for almost twenty years and died of cancer before he ever saw me play at the University of Tennessee. Growing up in Tennessee, every kid dreamed of playing for the Vols. When my dad told my grandfather that I was going to be a Volunteer, my grandfather said just one word: "Unbelievable."

Morgan (center) lining up to hike the
ball against the Dolphins
>> Rob Carr/AP/Shutterstock

I was a walk-on at Tennessee my freshman year, which meant that I wasn't offered a scholarship. But after winning the starting job at long snapper as a sophomore, I received a scholarship heading into the 2008 season. I started thirty-nine games for the Vols and even got invited to play in the Senior Bowl.

No team selected me in the 2010 NFL Draft. That wasn't surprising—teams don't often use a draft pick for a long snapper. I signed with Baltimore and began training camp competing for the starting job.

I'll always remember my first preseason game with the Ravens. I was resting on the sidelines while the defense was on the field. Suddenly, the players on the sidelines parted as Ray Lewis came off the field holding his hand against his chest. One of the trainers handed Ray a towel. Ray put it in his mouth and chomped down with his teeth. I then watched as the trainer took Ray's hand, popped his finger back into the socket, and taped it up. The Hall of Fame linebacker then ran back onto the field as if nothing had happened—and this was a *preseason* game! I thought, *What have I gotten myself into?* But it helped me see the commitment and toughness of NFL players.

Morgan playing tough, tackling Josh Cribbs hard enough to knock off Cribbs' helmet
>> Nick Wass/AP/Shutterstock

Later that season, after I had made the team, I tore the anterior cruciate ligament (ACL) in my left knee while blocking during a field goal. My mind flashed back to Ray Lewis and how he handled his injury. I had the trainer brace up my knee, and I played out the game knowing I needed immediate surgery. There was no way I was facing Ray Lewis and telling him I couldn't finish the game!

I also tore the ACL in my right knee in 2014. Being a long snapper comes with its dangers and pressures. When we were playing the Pittsburgh Steelers on Christmas Day in 2016, I snapped the ball too high on a field goal attempt in the second quarter. It was the first errant snap of my NFL career, which resulted in my team missing out on three points that we needed. I prayed a lot for the rest of that game—bullet prayers as I call them. Things like: "Lord, get me through this snap" and "I need your strength in this." It was a battle I hadn't faced since high school. My faith and my prayer life got me through this time of self-doubt, because my faith was in God.

> **MY FAITH AND MY PRAYER LIFE GOT ME THROUGH.**

FAMILY OF FAITH

My family always kept me grounded. I credit my parents with helping me to establish my faith. I accepted the Lord as my personal Savior when I was around eight years old. I remember sitting at our kitchen table and saying, "Jesus, I need you. I don't understand everything about you, but I know you died on the cross for my sins and I accept you as my Savior." My dad then walked into the kitchen, and I told him the decision I had just made.

I attended Evangelical Christian School in Cordova, Tennessee, where I played football and was the sports editor for our school's newspaper for two years. At 6'3" and 210 pounds, I handled long snapping duties for my high school team. I've since put on another thirty pounds to play in the NFL.

My parents not only modeled their Christian faith, they also modeled what a godly marriage looks like. I have carried that into my own marriage with my wife. She is a very faith-filled person and has been instrumental in me becoming the man I am today.

My wife and I read the Bible out loud from the time we first learned she was pregnant with our son, Daniel. We also began journaling notes and thoughts on the entire Bible, starting in Genesis. When my son is able to understand God's Word, we'll present him with a journal containing our thoughts and encouragements from each passage of Scripture. My dad did this for me. He gave me his journal as a present for my high school graduation. It's an amazing gift! It took so much dedication to read the entire Bible and write out his notes. I remember coming downstairs for school and seeing my dad in his chair early in the morning, doing his devotional and writing in the journal.

BLESSING **BEYOND** MEASURE

My favorite verse of the Bible Is Malachi 3:10: "'Bring the whole tithe into the storehouse, that there may be food in my house. Test me in this,' says the Lord Almighty, 'and see if I will not throw open the floodgates of heaven and pour out so much blessing that there will not be room enough to store it.'" This verse perfectly embodies my life up to this point. Every stage of my life has been a blessing, even through adversity. I have a great career, and I'm married to the best person ever for me and get to spend the rest of my life with her. God has blessed me not because of who I am or what I have done, but because he has put me in a position to exalt him. He has given me so much more than I have asked for or deserve.

All this may make it sound like I have it all together. *I don't*. I go astray at times. I've made plenty of mistakes and bad decisions. But I've always rededicated myself to the Lord when I fall, knowing that Jesus forgives me when I confess my sins and ask for forgiveness.

In my life today, I try to follow Christ and his example. I want to live my life how Christ lived his, so that others who don't know the gospel message, or think of it as a tired message, may see the attitude of a servant in me. I don't always understand right away the direction God is guiding me through the Holy Spirit, but I still try to follow.

When I went undrafted and first came into the league, I had to decide which team I would sign with. One team promised me a small signing bonus and a chance to compete at training camp. A second team offered me a much larger signing bonus and told me that the position was mine to lose. Baltimore, however, didn't offer me any signing bonus and told me I would have to compete with a seasoned veteran and try to win a roster spot on the team. I prayed over the decision and felt God lead me in the direction of the Ravens. On the surface, it didn't seem to make sense to choose Baltimore, but I felt God calling me here. Since that day, I have won a Super Bowl, been to the Pro Bowl, gotten married, become a father, played eight seasons in the NFL, and have a leadership position in the locker room.

My advice to everyone is to seek God's direction for your life. Pray that he will guide you, and then trust him. That doesn't mean you won't have adversity or that life will be perfect. I tore my ACL twice and still have beat out plenty of competition to keep my job. Trusting God does mean, however, that he will be with you, molding you into the person you were meant to be along the way. When you keep following God no matter what obstacle the world throws at you, your life will be unbelievable.

CHAPTER 23

Chris Brown/CSM/Shutterstock

ARTHUR MOATS
Don't Cross the Moats

@dabody52 1 cheek . . . 2 cheek hahaha, naw let me stop! Man thanks for being a great teammate and friend! Making it all the way from JMU to the NFL is a crazy accomplishment! Keep being you bro. You're a role model to everyone who knows you! #DontCrossTheMoats

James Madison University	Havelock, NC	Defensive End

The game had just begun between the Buffalo Bills and the Minnesota Vikings on December 5, 2010. Hall of Fame quarterback Brett Favre took the snap and rolled right on a 3rd-and-5 play for the Vikings. Rookie linebacker Arthur Moats flew around the edge, looking to tackle the quarterback. Seeing Favre move up in the pocket, Arthur changed direction, came back up the middle, and hit Favre just as he released the ball. The pass fluttered through the air and landed in the arms of a Bills player for an interception.

Favre was down, having landed on his right shoulder. At first Arthur didn't think much of it. He knew when he hit Favre that the quarterback had made a strange noise. But it was just a football play. The next week, however, Favre couldn't start the Vikings game against the New York Giants.

Favre's NFL record of starting 297 consecutive games had ended. Bills teammates started calling Arthur "Legend Killer." Arthur was just four years old when Favre's streak began. The Bills linebacker was twenty-two when he ended it with a massive hit. Favre learned early what numerous other NFL offensive players have come to realize over the years: Don't Cross the Moats!

I may be known for bringing people down on Sundays, but I want to be known for lifting people up. Both of my parents were pastors. While I was growing up in Portsmouth, Virginia, they helped me develop a heart for others. When I was eight, I remember going with my parents into lower income areas of my hometown on Sunday after church. We delivered free bread door to door to those who were less fortunate than us. The neighborhoods we went to were crime-infested places where murders happened. Drug dealers stood around on the street corners. Yet I could see the impact our kindness was having on these families. We didn't know their stories, but we wanted to give them food for free and asked for nothing in return. It taught me at an early age that if anyone is in a position to help others, they have an obligation to do it. It also made me feel grateful for the family I was born into.

Seeing all those families in need when I was a kid stuck with me. I didn't want to become a person in financial need myself. I decided that I needed to make sure everything I did was geared toward being successful. That meant doing better in school, practicing harder in sports, and staying out of trouble.

Because both of my parents were pastors, I had a knowledge and under-standing of who Christ was. I accepted Christ and was baptized at a young age. I thought I was doing all the right things by following the rules and trying my best.

I excelled on the high school football, basketball, track, wrestling, and soccer teams. During my senior year, I was a district champ in wrestling and the shot put in track and field. Even though I was good at those sports, I knew my future was in football. I had a bunch of Division I schools recruiting me, including Penn State and Virginia Tech. So it probably surprised some people that I chose to attend James Madison University, which definitely isn't a football powerhouse. Part of the decision came down to the coaches and players, part of it was JMU's political science program, and part of it was so I could be near my family. My parents got divorced when I was seventeen. Mom stayed in Portsmouth, and my dad moved to Maryland. Harrisonburg, Virginia, where JMU is located, was kind of in the middle.

Arthur (top center) with his family
>> Photo courtesy of Arthur Moats

I was all over the place during my freshman and sophomore years of college. I didn't go to Bible studies, and I stopped going to church. I wanted to be known as a "regular guy" instead of a "church guy." Tragically, during this time one of my close childhood friends was killed. His death caused me to ask myself where I would have spent eternity if it had been me who died instead of him. It was then that I realized I didn't have a personal walk with Jesus.

Arthur (rear right) works to tackle Richmond quarterback Nick Hicks while playing for James Madison

>> Pete Marovich/*Daily News-Record*/AP Images

I had been trying to be good using my own power. But following rules wouldn't save me. There was no way I could be "good enough" to earn my way to heaven. The only way to spend eternity with Jesus was to believe in him.

BACK TO THE BIBLE

During my junior year at James Madison, I began to avidly read my Bible and spend more time in prayer. Quickly, I saw my relationships with family and friends become healthier. I also did better in school and in sports. The correlation between my rededication to the Lord and my happiness and success was obvious.

My faith also sustained me during the NFL Draft. I'd graduated as one of the top defensive players in JMU history. During my senior year, I won the

Buck Buchanan Award, which goes to the top defensive player in the Division I Football Championship Subdivision. I was projected to be drafted in the third round. But I had to wait until the sixth round, when the Bills selected me.

I played in fifteen games for the Bills during my rookie year, but I didn't earn a starting position until late in the season. Over the next two seasons, I started fewer games. Although I was a starter in twelve games in 2013, each year the team drafted more linebackers in higher slots to try and replace me on the roster. The one consistency I had in my life was the Lord. My faith in him and his promises kept me focused on working hard.

Arthur (55) prevents a catch during a game against the Panthers
›› Mike McCarn/AP/Shutterstock

After four seasons in Buffalo, I signed with the Steelers and had a solid first season with the Black and Gold. This success and an opening in their linebacking unit led the Steelers to sign me to a sizeable three-year contract. With this success also came a challenge: staying humble! It's easy to remain humble when you don't have money. But when you get a big contract, everything changes. I had to remain true to my morals and values and not let my financial status change who I was. I needed to lean on Christ to help me understand that I represent him, and not let my ego get the best of me.

As a Christian, people are watching my walk and making judgments about who Christ is based on the way I carry myself. Ultimately, if I'm looking in the mirror, I want the reflection to be Christ-like. When I wake up in the morning, my prayer is: *Lord, I want to be more like you, be more righteous, and be as close to you as I can be.* The Bible says if we are lukewarm for him, he will spit us out. I want God to say to me, "Well done, good and faithful servant." By no means am I perfect. I fall short all the time. But I always want to stay pointed in the right direction.

Part of that is giving back to the community and being involved in ministry work. I don't do it for the notoriety. I give because it's the right thing to do. My parents taught me that, and God commands it in his Word. During my career with Buffalo and Pittsburgh, I've been nominated for and received some of the highest community service awards in the National Football League. In 2013, I received the Ed Block Courage Award, given to the player on each club who is voted by their teammates as a role model of inspiration, sportsmanship, and courage. That same season, I was the Bills' nominee for the Walter Payton Man of the Year Award for

> I ALWAYS WANT TO STAY POINTED IN THE RIGHT DIRECTION.

excellence on and off the field. Later, in 2016, I was Pittsburgh's nominee for the Art Rooney Sportsmanship Award and the Walter Payton Man of the Year Award. I also won the Chief Award, which is given to the Steeler the team feels best works with the media during the good times and the bad times.

Like I said, I act the way I do to honor God, not win awards. We should all think before we act. One wrong decision can have serious consequences for your schooling, your job, your family, or even for your life. It can be as simple as, *Should I study or not?* Or, *Should I listen to my parents or not?* Or it can be as serious as, *Should I join my friends in something illegal?* I've been on both sides of the fence. Don't act in anger or without thinking about the potential consequences. Ask the Lord what is the right decision, and he will help you.

And if you don't have a personal relationship with Jesus, I encourage you to accept Christ into your life and become a child of God. Make that decision today. It starts with a prayer like this:

"Jesus, I believe only you can save me and forgive me of my sins. And I know I've made mistakes in my life. Thank you for dying for me. I accept your gift of salvation and commit my life to following you. Help me to live for you. Amen.

If you just prayed that prayer, tell somebody! Tell a parent, a pastor, a friend, or the person who gave you this book. Tweet at one of the players featured in this book. We will definitely respond.

A radio announcer in Buffalo came up with the phrase Don't Cross the Moats! But as I sit back and think about it, it's really Jesus' death on a *cross* that we should be paying attention to.

SLOW **TO** ANGER

My favorite Bible verse is packed with advice I can use every day of my life. James 1:19–20 reads: "Everyone should be quick to listen, slow to speak and slow to become angry, because human anger does not produce the righteousness that God desires." Too many times, things said out of anger or a lack of understanding have devastating impact on relationships. Angry words can ruin lives. Avoid that mistake by taking the time to listen and not just swiftly react.

CHAPTER 24

DERRICK MORGAN

God's Plan, Not Mine

@dmorg91 Man, I find myself thinking about that trip we took to New York a lot. Haha! Too much of a blast. I'm glad you in this book too bro. We def gotta represent PA! Keep leading and being a role model! I seen the desires of your eyes to be great when I was in Tennessee. Keep God 1st and it will happen!

Georgia Tech	Lancaster, PA	Linebacker

Every year leading up to the NFL Draft, teams face a big challenge. They have to project how a player will perform in the NFL—not just the following year, but in five to eight years in the future. Today's college phenom may become an NFL bust. Drafting wrong with a top pick could ruin a season or put an organization on a downward spiral. Every team wants its top draft choice to be a game-changer.

Derrick Morgan was the Tennessee Titans' first-round choice in 2010, drafted sixteenth overall. The 6'5", 260-pound defensive end recorded his first NFL sack in his first game. However, in his fourth game, Derrick tore the ACL in his left knee. He worked hard to rehabilitate the injury, making his first career start in the seventh game of the 2011 season. Since then, he has been playing the way teams want to see from a top draft pick. He can play on either side of the defensive line and at outside linebacker. Following eight years in Tennessee, his statistics keep getting better and better. In 2016, Derrick notched nine sacks and a team-leading fifty-six quarterback pressures. He followed that up with 7.5 sacks during the 2017 season. His road hasn't been smooth, but he's now faithfully committed to following God's plan.

I thought I'd reached the pinnacle of life when I was drafted into the NFL. It was everything I'd hoped for. My junior year at Georgia Tech had been filled with highlights: 12.5 sacks, Atlantic Coast Conference Defensive Player of the Year, All-American honors, and our team won the ACC Championship. After the season, I decided to forego my senior year and entered the draft. When I was picked sixteenth overall, I thought I had it made. I signed a six-year contract and was getting reps at defensive end. However, in only the fourth game of my career, I tore my ACL. This led to the first of three surgeries in two years on my left knee.

Coming back from injury each time was difficult and painful. But through these trials, I came to realize I had placed my whole identity in the game of football. Football had become my idol. Without it, I felt like I'd be nothing.

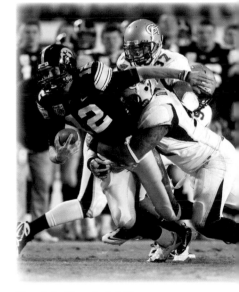

Derrick (front right) tackling Iowa's Ricky Stanzi during the Orange Bowl

» J. Pat Carter/AP/Shutterstock

That's when I decided that I needed to put my identity in Christ alone. Football was fleeting—God is eternal. When I got grounded in my faith, I knew that no matter what happened in this life, my identity rested in being a man of God.

From a young age, I had an understanding of who God was. I was raised by a single mom in Lancaster, Pennsylvania. I give her credit with instilling solid values and principles into my life. She ensured I was in church every Sunday. She set my foundation and was my primary role model. Sometimes I can't believe how much she sacrificed for me. Even with the busy schedule of a single parent, she made sure I got to every sports practice and she came to all my games.

Derrick (91) rushing the Buccaneers'
quarterback Jameis Winston

›› Jeff Haynes/AP/Shutterstock

Back in those days I thought I could do anything on the football field. As a senior at Coatesville Area High School, I was named league Defensive Player of the Year and first-team all-state. I had forty-seven tackles and seven sacks at the defensive end position, and I rushed for 523 yards and eight touchdowns as a running back. Although I knew about God and followed Christian principles, I didn't have a personal relationship with God until adversity reared its head in my first NFL season. I had spent years trying to force things to go my way. It was all about my own plans for life. That mindset led me to hit dead end after dead end. Once I accepted God's plan for my life, though, I came to realize it was so much better than my own plan. I started trusting his will more than my own.

GOOD **THOUGHT**

Philippians 4:8 is my favorite Bible verse, because it reminds me where to focus my mental energy. The verse says, "Finally, brothers and sisters, whatever is true, whatever is noble, whatever is right, whatever is pure, whatever is lovely, whatever is admirable—if anything is excellent or praiseworthy—think about such things." Thoughts are powerful. This verse gives me guidelines on where my thoughts should be and instructs me not to focus on my failures. I don't focus on negativity, but instead think about the positive things in my life.

Since then, my faith has helped provide me a better perspective on dealing with the adversities within the game of football. Football isn't an easy sport to play. It comes with a lot of physical and mental stresses. Hard work and perseverance are required to succeed and meet your goals. My faith challenges me to continue through difficult times and keeps me from giving up at the first hint of failure.

I can honestly say that being a Christian is the most important thing in my life. It starts with believing in God and believing in Jesus. But being a Christian

IT WAS ALL ABOUT MY OWN PLANS FOR LIFE. THAT MINDSET LED ME TO HIT DEAD END AFTER DEAD END.

also means you actually follow his teachings and his commandments. Now don't get me wrong, that's much easier said than done. But, ultimately, you need to deny your own ways and imitate the character of Jesus.

Derrick (center) at a surprise appearance, after speaking with local teens about his experiences

>> Photo courtesy of Derrick Morgan

There are a lot of distractions in this world. A lot of people and a lot of things promise happiness and prosperity. I thought I had it figured out in high school. In several national rankings, I was rated the top football prospect coming out of the state of Pennsylvania. In three years at Georgia Tech, I made a big enough name for myself that I was drafted in the first round. But I found the only true happiness and peace you will find in this world is in the Bible and in following Jesus. Don't rely on things of this world that are here today and gone tomorrow. Put your faith in God and live your life for him. I did, and I discovered that the life he has given me is better than anything I could have imagined for myself. I'm thankful God got ahold of my life, because it's all about his plan, not mine.

CHAPTER 25

John Bazemore/AP/
Shutterstock

BEN GARLAND
Strength Through Weakness

@BenGarland63 Man, I feel like we both were given the short end of the stick at the beginning of our careers. And you know we always go hard!! From undrafted 2 starter!! Keep going bro. You have made it so far, and you are definitely an inspiration to me. #WPMOY #AirForce

| Air Force Academy | Grand Junction, CO | Offensive Guard |

The A-10 Thunderbolt II is one tough fighter plane. Nicknamed the "Warthog" and the "Tankbuster," it's the only aircraft in the Air Force specifically designed to help defend troops on the ground. The A-10 is highly maneuverable at low speeds and in low altitudes. Its seven-barrel Gatling gun is the heaviest automatic cannon ever mounted to an airplane. It can also hold missiles and laser-guided bombs. Pilots of these airplanes require hundreds of hours of training and nerves of steel.

When Ben Garland graduated from the United States Air Force Academy in 2010, he had a difficult decision to make: fly the A-10 or play in the NFL. Through four years of hard work, he had earned a coveted spot in the fighter pilot training program. As a 6'5", 308-pound defensive lineman for the Air Force Academy's Falcons football team, Ben had started thirty-four games and terrorized opposing offenses. And with 115 tackles and 11.5 sacks, he had gained the attention of the NFL. It wasn't an easy decision. But ultimately, Ben pursued his dream of playing in the NFL.

No path to the NFL is easy. If mine was plotted out, it'd be anything but a straight line. It'd look more like a windy, switchback-filled trail that climbs up 14,410 feet to the top of Pikes Peak in Colorado Springs.

**Ben as a child, wearing
his favorite jersey**

›› Photo courtesy of Ben Garland

In 2010, the Denver Broncos signed me as an undrafted free agent. I was placed on the NFL's reserve/military list to serve out my two-year military commitment after graduating from the United States Air Force. The Broncos released me on August 31, 2012, only to re-sign me to the practice squad the next day.

Then in 2013, Denver released me again. However, I was again quickly re-signed to the team. I kept working. I did whatever I could to get on the field. Finally, in 2014, I stepped onto an NFL field during the regular season. Yeah, November 9, 2014, to be exact. That was special for a couple reasons. First, it marked my successful switch from defensive lineman to offensive lineman. I'd entered the league on the D-line, but I had more opportunity to play

O-line for the Broncos, so I made the move. But this game was also special because it was against the hated Oakland Raiders. I grew up in Grand Junction, Colorado, as a huge Broncos fan. Now I was lacing up my cleats against a team I'd despised and desperately wanted to beat. And we did: 41–17.

After four years with the Broncos, the team released me for the last time in 2015. Atlanta picked me up four days later. I was a Falcon again! Except not an Army Falcon, but a Falcon in the NFL. Since joining the Falcons, I've played in a Super Bowl, started on the offensive line, and even scored a safety in a playoff game against Seattle. That day was January 14, 2017. I came into the game on D-line with the Seahawks backed against their goal line. Seattle quarterback Russell Wilson got tangled with one of his offensive linemen. He went to the ground just as I beat my man, and I dove on him for two points! That's a play I definitely won't forget.

Ben lining up as a Falcon against the Denver Broncos
>> Jack Dempsey/AP/Shutterstock

As I look back on my NFL career so far, I've lined up at tight end, fullback, center, left and right offensive guard, defensive tackle, and defensive end. That doesn't even count the hundreds of special teams plays where I've blocked for field goals and punts or ran downfield to make a tackle. To tell the truth, I'd play punter, quarterback, or safety as long as it would help my team win and get me on the field.

I've always loved sports, but I haven't always been the best athlete.

If you've ever played kickball during recess at school, you've probably experienced standing in a line waiting to be picked by the captains. The kids who could run the fastest or kick the farthest always got picked first. Then there were the kids without the obvious physical abilities. These kids needed to prove themselves to gain the acceptance of the other players. That was me. I was never the biggest, the strongest, the smartest, or the fastest. I had to work twice as hard as anyone else did. Growing up, I felt like an underdog. But an underdog with God on his side isn't an underdog at all. Deuteronomy 20:1–4 states, "When you go to war against your enemies and see horses and chariots and an army greater than yours, do not be afraid of them . . . Do not panic or be terrified by them. For the Lord your God is the one who goes with you to fight for you against your enemies to give you victory."

Ben singing carols to veterans at the Atlanta VA Medical Center

›› David Goldman/AP/Shutterstock

I grew up in a very strong Christian household. Those verses encouraged me to take the field with confidence—no matter how big the opponent. I knew that Christ would strengthen me and fight for me. I also know it's God who has helped me overcome injuries and obstacles, and the struggles of switching from team to team and position to position, to get me where I am today.

I came to know Christ at a very young age. My parents didn't force religion on me. They let me decide on my own. They also let me choose when I would be baptized. It was important to me to show the world I was serious about my faith.

The most important relationship anyone can have is their relationship with God and Jesus Christ. True success is found in a day-after-day attempt to draw closer to God. Being a Christian doesn't just mean trying to be Christ-like; it also means building relationships with others to show them what God has done in your life. This world needs people who shine God's light, because so many others

I HAD TO WORK TWICE AS HARD AS ANYONE ELSE DID.

are hurting or struggling. That's why I make time to visit children in the hospital or speak at events that bring people hope. I can't do anything in my own strength, but I've seen God use my efforts to accomplish great deeds, impact lives, and do things I never imagined possible.

RENEWED STRENGTH

My faith in God has also given me the strength to never give up and to accomplish my goals. From age five, I promised myself that I'd play at the Air Force Academy and then for the Denver Broncos.

My grandfather, retired Colonel Hugh Garland, was a hero to me growing up. I wanted to follow in his footsteps and attend the Air Force Academy. I also wanted to be a man of integrity, like he was. Not only did he serve our country, he served the Lord. At times when it felt like I was stuck on the practice squad, I remembered to keep trusting God. That's what my grandfather would've done.

Even switching positions was a huge leap of faith. Playing offensive line and defensive line require totally different skills and mindsets. At the start of the 2014 season with the Broncos, I was fighting for a starting spot on the offensive line. During our last preseason game against the Dallas Cowboys, I suffered a high ankle sprain during one of the game's first plays. The pain was excruciating, but I knew I couldn't quit. Everybody in the NFL plays through pain. I didn't want to let my teammates down. I ended up having one of my best games in what would eventually become my breakout season.

One of Ben's (33) big plays against the Academy of Colorado while playing for the Air Force

>> US Air Force photo/John Van Winkle

It's through hardships, times of weakness, and persecution that God really shows his strength. It's like what the Bible says in Isaiah 40:31: "Those who hope in the Lord will renew their strength. They will soar on wings like eagles; they will run and not grow weary, they will walk and not be faint." That verse is a constant source of strength for me. There are times in practice or during games where teammates have said, "Man, there must be something special in your water! You never get tired!"

Trust me, there's nothing in *my* water. It's the living water that comes from Christ that pushes me through when other players are falling apart, getting tired, or quitting.

Whenever I get the chance to talk with people, I like to ask them, "If you believed you couldn't fail, what would you attempt to do?" It's a question that can change the course of your life. It's certainly changed mine. Every obstacle I've faced, I've known I can overcome because of my faith in Christ. After all, if God is with me, who can stand against me? Right?!? I know you've heard that before. But hearing and believing are two different things. You have to truly believe it.

Hard work will defeat talent every time talent refuses to work. That's what I've seen throughout my life. Plenty of guys I played against in high school and college had more talent than I did. But they never made it to the NFL, because they didn't put in the work. Working hard will make you strong. Effort will take you farther. But never forget: To accomplish your big dreams, you need to find the strength that can only be discovered in weakness.

PERFECT **POWER**

Life can be filled with fear, struggle, and weakness. It's the nature of living in a fallen world. How we deal with trials and tribulations defines us as a person. When I face hardships, I always stand by my favorite Bible verse from 2 Corinthians 12:9: "But he said to me, 'My grace is sufficient for you, for my power is made perfect in weakness.' Therefore I will boast all the more gladly about my weaknesses, so that Christ's power may rest on me."

We all have weakness. But in our weakness, God can show his perfect power. Where we have the greatest need and biggest hurt is where he shines through the most.

ABOUT THE AUTHORS

Steven Johnson Jr. is an American football linebacker who has played six seasons in the National Football League. He is also the CEO and founder of the Faith Motivated Foundation, a charity designed to empower youth by demonstrating how to set and achieve goals while also seeking to educate and model a healthy lifestyle by motivating good choices through Christ. Steven has overcome insurmountable odds his entire life. He is the definition of diligence, patience, and perseverance. Check out the Faith Motivated Foundation at www.faithmotivated.org

Paul Cartwright and his wife, Fay, are co-owners of Sports Celebrity Marketing, S.C.M. Inc. As sports fans and believers in Jesus Christ, this book became an exciting family undertaking. Paul was honored to write about the grace that God has given to these elite athletes to use their sport as a platform. Sports Celebrity Marketing, S.C.M. Inc. is a full-service sports agency doing business in both the United States and Canada. Its roster includes personalities from all major sports, including baseball, hockey, football, and more.